HAUNTED HOMES

QUICK TAKES: MOVIES AND POPULAR CULTURE

Quick Takes: Movies and Popular Culture is a series offering succinct overviews and high-quality writing on cutting-edge themes and issues in film studies. Authors offer both fresh perspectives on new areas of inquiry and original takes on established topics.

SERIES EDITORS:

Gwendolyn Audrey Foster is Willa Cather Professor of English and teaches film studies in the Department of English at the University of Nebraska, Lincoln.

Wheeler Winston Dixon is the James Ryan Endowed Professor of Film Studies and professor of English at the University of Nebraska, Lincoln.

Rebecca Bell-Metereau,
Transgender Cinema

Blair Davis,
Comic Book Movies

Jonna Eagle,
War Games

Lester D. Freidman,
Sports Movies

Desirée J. Garcia,
The Movie Musical

Steven Gerrard,
The Modern British Horror Film

Barry Keith Grant,
Monster Cinema

Julie Grossman,
The Femme Fatale

Daniel Herbert,
Film Remakes and Franchises

Ian Olney, *Zombie Cinema*

Valérie K. Orlando,
New African Cinema

Carl Plantinga,
Alternative Realities

Stephen Prince, *Digital Cinema*

Dahlia Schweitzer,
L.A. Private Eyes

Dahlia Schweitzer,
Haunted Homes

Steven Shaviro,
Digital Music Videos

David Sterritt,
Rock 'n' Roll Movies

John Wills, *Disney Culture*

Haunted Homes

DAHLIA SCHWEITZER

RUTGERS UNIVERSITY PRESS

New Brunswick, Camden, and Newark, New Jersey, and London

Library of Congress Cataloging-in-Publication Data
Names: Schweitzer, Dahlia, author.
Title: Haunted homes / Dahlia Schweitzer.
Description: New Brunswick, New Jersey : Rutgers University
Press, [2021]. | Series: Quick takes: movies and popular culture |
Includes bibliographical references and index.
Identifiers: LCCN 2020042806 | ISBN 9781978807730
(paperback) | ISBN 9781978807747 (cloth) | ISBN 9781978807754
(epub) | ISBN 9781978807761 (mobi) | ISBN 9781978807778 (pdf)
Subjects: LCSH: Haunted houses in motion pictures. |
Suburbs in motion pictures. | Suburban life in motion pictures. |
Suburban life—United States.
Classification: LCC PN1995.9.H367 S39 2021 |
DDC 791.43/675—dc23
LC record available at https://lccn.loc.gov/2020042806

A British Cataloging-in-Publication record for this book is
available from the British Library.

∞ The paper used in this publication meets the requirements of
the American National Standard for Information Sciences—
Permanence of Paper for Printed Library Materials,
ANSI Z39.48-1992.

www.rutgersuniversitypress.org

Manufactured in the United States of America

CONTENTS

Introduction   1

1 The Suburbs   6

2 The Suburban Gothic   29

3 Gender, Horror, and the Home   61

4 Race, Horror, and the Home   114

Conclusion   148

Acknowledgments   161

Further Reading   163

Works Cited   165

Index   173

HAUNTED HOMES

INTRODUCTION

Even serial killers live next door to somebody.
                                                    —*Summer of 84*

Haunted houses feel as much a part of Halloween as pumpkins and costumes. It can be hard to remember where you first saw a haunted house or how old you were the first time you went inside one. They are ubiquitous and generic, commercialized, commodified, and caricatured. Because of their ability to scale up the horror from kid-friendly "eyeballs" in a bowl all the way to actual violence, as in the case of McKamey Manor in Tennessee and Alabama, haunted houses continue to draw in crowds looking for a thrill.

A haunted *home* is something different entirely. Unlike the term "house," which describes a building's style and purpose, the word "home" refers to something more personal and emotional. The concept of "home" directly involves the people who live inside, whereas "house" merely refers to the structure itself, to the walls and the way they are put together. A home does not need to be

1

a house; it can be an apartment or a boat or a trailer or a cardboard box. A home is where someone feels as though they belong, where they feel safe, where they feel most truly themselves.

Many discussions of horror films—and specifically those set in the domestic arena—tend to be ahistorical, treating modern-day narratives as though they are simply a continuation of European Gothic novels from the eighteenth century. However, this simplification does a disservice to the particular nuances of the haunted home narrative, a style of storytelling uniquely tied to the evolution of the suburban United States and the suburban home specifically.

For almost a century, Hollywood has been delivering memorable portrayals of evil homes full of lingering trauma, malevolent ghosts, and sometimes even portals to hell. While Paul Leni's *The Cat and the Canary* (1927), in which a family is terrorized in a creepy mansion, may have been the first film to establish the look and feel of the "haunted home," other films—such as James Whale's aptly titled *The Old Dark House* (1932), in which travelers taking solace from rain are terrified by the residents of yet another creepy mansion, as well as Lewis Allen's *The Uninvited* (1944), in which a brother and sister impulsively buy an abandoned house, only to discover that it comes with ghosts—kept expanding its parameters.

More recently, the success of Mike Flanagan's Netflix series *The Haunting of Hill House* (2018), loosely based on Shirley Jackson's novel of the same name, in which a family revisits the haunted home of their youth, as well as movies like Ari Aster's *Hereditary* (2018), in which a family is haunted by evil spirits, demonstrates the continued appeal of watching sinister forces encroaching on the domestic front.

Sometimes these forces are literal, sometimes they are confined to nightmares and dreamscapes, but the end result remains the same: home is where the horror is. This premise is all the more remarkable since homes are traditionally equated with safety and sanctuary. After all, when do you feel more safe than when you return home, letting the door close behind you, the outside world kept at a distance? However, the template of the "haunted home narrative" plays precisely on the paradox of that premise, bringing fear into the otherwise placid home, perverting the satisfying accomplishment of the American dream with abject terror and financial—if not also physical—ruin.

But why? On the one hand, we have persistent messaging that suburbia is bliss, full of happy families, green lawns, and well-adjusted children, even if also a bit boring and homogeneous. On the other hand, however, we have the stubborn appeal of movies and television shows

determined to show us that that bliss is a lie, that true horror begins (and ends) at home, and that safety will never
be achieved until the family house—that ultimate indica-
tor of American success and status—is shrinking in the
rearview mirror.

This book examines not only the growth of the suburban neighborhood but also its long-term impact on
American identity and the American family as depicted
in US film and television. Suburbia is not just an architectural choice or geographic preference. Suburbia estab-
lishes and reinforces specific modes of behavior, not all
of which come with messages of opportunity and hope.
It shifts focus to the family while, at the same time, isolating the family—from other people and the individual
members from each other. It is a fundamental rethinking
of the relationship between city and home, between husband and wife, between job and family, between private
and public space. While most of the texts discussed in
this book are set in stereotypical American suburbia, not
all are. For example, the film and television adaptations of
Shirley Jackson's novel *The Haunting of Hill House* are set
in an isolated nineteenth-century mansion rather than in a
modern suburban home, the haunted homes in *The Innocents* (Jack Clayton, 1961) and *The Witch* (Robert Eggers,
2015) are situated in presuburban pasts, and a handful
of movies discussed in this book are located outside the

United States, such as *The Uninvited* (Lewis Allen, 1944) and *The Babadook* (Jennifer Kent, 2014). I have opted to include these films for the effective ways they depict my arguments. For instance, once you understand how the family is literally isolated in a nineteenth-century mansion, it is easier to understand and observe more contemporary incarnations of this same isolation.

As Davey Armstrong (Graham Verchere) explains via voice-over in the movie *Summer of 84* (François Simard, Anouk Whissell, and Yoann-Karl Whissell, 2018), "Just past the manicured lawns and friendly waves, inside any house, even the one next door, anything could be happening, and you'd never know. . . . It all might seem normal and routine, but the truth is the suburbs are where the craziest shit happens." This book is about that crazy shit and what it tells us about ourselves.

1

THE SUBURBS

In order to understand the terror that so often accompanies portrayals of suburbia in contemporary horror, it is important to understand the creation of suburbia itself. Suburbia did not evolve gradually or organically. It was not a nurturing response to the grimness of the Industrial Revolution or the horrors of war. Rather, it was a carefully constructed house of cards engineered via government policy and racist strategy, built on precarious legal agreements, all of which would coalesce to form (on the surface) rows and rows of uniform homes, each promising opportunity and hope for those who were lucky enough to buy in, while (below the surface) a web of oppression, racism, cruelty, and financial risk lurked and festered.

So, if not organic, from where did the suburbs come? A relatively recent American invention, they can be linked specifically to the end of World War II. Millions of soldiers returning home from Europe received incentives—financial and otherwise—to relocate their burgeoning families to the rapidly expanding suburbs, which were being built and fleshed out through careful government and corporate strategy. For instance, between 1948 and 1958, eleven million new suburban homes were built, with an astonishing 83 percent of all population growth during the 1950s taking place in those new neighborhoods (Murphy 6). A shift this radical would have countless repercussions, not only on individual residents but also on the American way of life.

The Industrial Revolution, which took place in the United States roughly from 1790 to 1840, drastically changed how people worked as well as how (and where) they lived. Responsible not only for the shift from hand production to machine production, as well as from an agricultural society to an industrial one, the Industrial Revolution spurred massive economic and population growth. This growth happened almost exclusively in cities that would be flooded by people looking for work and trying to survive, quite the shift from the abundance of space and land that had existed in the United States during the eighteenth century and before.

To say the infrastructure in these newly exploding cities was poorly planned is an understatement. Well into the twentieth century, both living and working conditions were dreadful. Since there was an endless supply of potential workers, factories could treat their employees as disposable because they literally were. There was always someone willing to work more hours for less pay. And if long hours and demeaning salaries were not bad enough, it was common for workers to be injured or killed on the job. Home life was not much better. Poorly constructed tenement apartments housed as many people as could fit, inhabitants living without windows, heating, or even plumbing. Sewage systems were often nonexistent. Unsurprisingly, diseases such as cholera and typhus spread rapidly. Is it any surprise that anyone who could afford to fled the cities?

However, it was not just oppressed and exploited workers who wanted to leave city centers. Employers and union leaders realized that skilled workers needed better housing options. As Dolores Hayden explains in her book *Redesigning the American Dream: The Future of Housing, Work, and Family Life*, employers came up with a plan to "miniaturize and mass produce the Victorian patriarchal, suburban businessman's dwelling" (33). However, this plan was not fueled by altruistic motives. Rather, employers wanted to lock down workers, discouraging them from leaving or going on strike, by getting them to invest their savings in homes (Hayden 33). The employees owned the home, but the employers owned the employees. Once a family is financially committed to a house, the primary breadwinner is less likely to quit a job. In general, people are more willing to put up with less-than-ideal working conditions because of the lack of flexibility demanded by homeownership. Employers recognized this and took advantage.

In the early twentieth century, real estate companies and government agencies still believed people were not buying enough homes, so in 1917, the National Association of Real Estate Boards launched the "Own Your Own Home" campaign, which would later be taken over by the US Department of Labor. The first federal program to advocate homeownership—even if it did not provide any actual financial incentives—was a promotional campaign that linked owning a home to true patriotism. This strategy set the course for the belief not only that owning a home is a rite of passage but that owning a home is an integral part of the American dream. Susan Saegert explains that homeownership is pushed as such a "basic American fantasy" that it has "fed right into the ethos of the United States" and, in fact, "become an aspect of being an American" (qtd. in DePalma). Going even further, Samira Kawash argues that it is not just an aspect of being an American but "the supreme achievement of American adulthood," despite the "array of subsidies, preferences, and prejudices" necessary to make home-ownership a reality for many (185).

In 1922, Herbert Hoover, then secretary of commerce for the United States, equated increased homeownership with a more stable nation. As a result, he made home-ownership one of his priorities by taking over the "Own Your Own Home" campaign. Thanks to him and various related campaigns, homeownership did increase during the 1920s, but this increase was only temporary. The Great Depression caused a rise in home foreclosures and a decline in homeownership rates. Many people lost their savings due to the lack of federal deposit insurance. The number of mortgages issued plummeted, as did the number of people owning homes. In response, Hoover, by this point president of the United States, created the Home Loan Bank System to help financial institutions suffering under the growing weight of people defaulting on their mortgages. This was only the beginning of government intervention in the domestic real estate market.

Hoover's successor, President Franklin Delano Roosevelt, further increased the ability of the government to intervene in the mortgage market with the creation of the Home Owners' Loan Corporation (HOLC) in 1933. The primary purpose of the HOLC was to transform short-term mortgages (whose owners were at risk of defaulting) into long-term mortgages that were government subsidized, thus reducing the number of homeowners who were forced to default. In principle, this was a good thing, and the HOLC was able to help many homeowners refinance and keep their homes. Unfortunately, the new longer-term loans created a problem: banks were often left starved for cash. In order to allow banks to offer even more home loans, the federal government had to intervene yet again, creating another government institution. The Federal National Mortgage Association (Fannie Mae) bought mortgages from cash-starved banks, thus enabling the banks to offer loans to more prospective homeowners.

Another government institution established to facilitate homeownership was the Federal Housing Administration (FHA). Created in 1934, just a couple of years into the Great Depression, the FHA aimed to improve housing standards nationwide. Specifically, the FHA meant to make it easier for certain groups of people to buy homes by making the mortgage process more accessible. The then-current protocol—paying 50 percent down on signing and then paying the rest off within five to ten years—was out of reach for many Americans, so the FHA began offering federally backed insurance for mortgages to reduce the risk that banks were carrying. This, in turn, enabled banks to offer longer-term mortgages with lower interest rates and reduced down payments, making it easier for more people to qualify for homeownership.

The message is clear: most Americans do not buy homes with cash in hand. They are only able to become homeowners because of a complex system of government institutions working together to make homeownership more accessible for those who are deemed deserving. At the same time, these institutions also made some home-owners vulnerable precisely by facilitating the accessibility of homeownership. Many homeowners got locked into mortgages (and homes) they could not technically afford as a result of a variety of questionable practices. And this element of suburbia—spending more than you can afford to fit in—has proved pivotal to haunted home narratives.

Despite all this maneuvering to make homes more accessible, the federal government realized that many military veterans and their families would still have nowhere to go once World War II was over. Determined to improve on the "$60 and a ticket home" that veterans had received following World War I, government and corporate agendas united to solve this shortage and to stimulate suburban growth and industry. In 1944, President Roosevelt signed into law the GI Bill of Rights, officially known as the Servicemen's Readjustment Act, to reward veterans for their service.

The GI Bill offered veterans government-backed, low-interest, long-term (twenty-five to thirty years) fixed-rate mortgages with zero or low down payments. The intention was that veterans would be able to purchase homes whose values would rise, providing the veterans (and therefore the country) with economic stability. These mortgages applied to new homes in the suburbs, as opposed to urban areas, because the government specifically wanted to stimulate suburban growth. These mortgages allowed all but the poorest veterans to buy—as long as they bought the right kind of home in the right kind of area and as long as they were white. African American veterans were usually denied mortgages and excluded from many suburban neighborhoods even if they could afford to move.

The FHA enforced the uniform nature of suburban homes by lowering the value of houses that did not conform to their basic design norms (Hayden 43). It operated with the belief that neighborhoods with similar homes tended to be more stable and that, ideally, property values should all be within a close range. Conveniently, it is also much cheaper and easier to build homes that share similar designs. Levittown—actually the name for several separate developments created by William Levitt and his company in states like New York, Pennsylvania, and New Jersey—exemplified this strategy. When Levitt, who had served in the navy, returned home after the war, he saw opportunity in the housing shortage that confronted him and many other veterans. He proposed using techniques of mass-production that he had learned while constructing military housing, combined with assembly-line procedures adopted from automobile manufacturers, to help meet the demand for new homes in the United States. Levitt & Sons began building homes specifically for army veterans and their families, famously building a (more or less) identical house every sixteen minutes during peak productivity (Marshall). Within four years, there were over seventeen thousand homes in Levittown, Long Island, alone. Companies like Levitt & Sons went on to build thousands of similar homes in planned communities—communities without any industry or historical tradition—throughout the United States, creating entirely new towns and an entirely new way of life.

Lewis Mumford, in his book *The City in History: Its Origins, Its Transformations, and Its Prospects*, scathingly describes these new neighborhoods as "uniform, unidentifiable houses, lined up inflexibly, at uniform distances, on uniform roads, in a treeless communal waste" (299). Mumford goes on to describe the residents of these houses as "people of the same class, the same income, the same age group, witnessing the same television performances, eating the same tasteless pre-fabricated foods, from the same freezers, conforming in every outward and inward respect to a common mold manufactured in the central metropolis" (299). Some critiques of this new way of life satirized the mind-numbing conformity, such as Ira Levin's best-selling novel *The Stepford Wives* (published in 1972 and adapted into two films) about a suburban neighborhood full of submissive housewives who are actually robots. Nonetheless, uniform was equated with stable, and stable was equated with desirable; and so the uniform suburbs kept growing in size and popularity.

In 1946, the average price of a suburban home—two bedrooms, one bathroom, a living room, and a kitchen—came to about $5,150. With an attractive no-interest (or low-interest) loan, mortgage payments might be under $30 a month. Locking in a home for such a low price promised prosperity and possibility, both for Americans and for the United States. For those who were lucky enough to get a mortgage, the suburbs beckoned. According to the US Census Bureau, by 1950, 55 percent of Americans owned their own home.

Unfortunately, this prosperity did not last. Between 1970 and 1982, inflation skyrocketed. Housing prices more than doubled, with average housing prices leaping from $28,700 to $87,600 (Hayden 56). Bankruptcies, job losses, and soaring gas prices, combined with less available land and stricter building restrictions, did not help. The growth of the earlier decades had been replaced with stagnation and unemployment, increased use of technology rendering many jobs (and those who were qualified to perform those jobs) irrelevant. The amount of American debt tied up in residential mortgages increased from $661 billion in 1967 to $1,172 billion in 1982 (Hayden 57).

Just as the thirty million children born during the initial period of suburban expansion were ready to buy homes themselves, housing had grown out of reach, metaphorically and literally. In order to find affordable homes, people had to drive farther and farther from city centers. Aaron Klein, policy director for the Center on Regulation and Markets, describes this concept as "drive until you qualify." Not only did increased travel time exacerbate the isolation for those who were stuck in the car as well as those who were stuck at home, but growing transportation costs—such as the rising cost of gasoline—also contributed directly to foreclosures. If you were lucky enough to have a home of your own, the economic struggles of the 1970s still posed a problem. Keeping up with payments for a house you already bought became a challenge thanks to predatory lending practices and skyrocketing interest rates. Nonetheless, the pressure to buy remained intense. People kept buying homes as they remained the best way to build equity, wealth, and credit. The suburbs, which had represented "only a fourth of the country in 1950, and still just a third in 1960, encompassed more than half of America by 1990" (Kruse 259).

Homeownership prices continued to increase throughout the 1990s. Since mortgage interest rates were low and home prices were increasing, buyers would borrow large sums of money with low monthly payments. Homeownership seemed like such a solid financial investment that lenders were willing to lend money against the value of a home, allowing existing homeowners to take out second mortgages, turning their homes' equity into cash to finance additional expenses. While this seemed good in the short term, it represented disaster in the long term.

In the early years of the twenty-first century, there was a dramatic increase in predatory mortgage lending, especially among minorities. Predatory lending usually describes risky loans, with excessive fees, higher-than-normal interest rates, and/or particularly difficult payment obligations offered to consumers with poor credit who could not qualify for more traditional loans. These loans are often offered with little to no documentation required, allowing borrowers to qualify for loans they could not otherwise afford. To make things worse, the required information on loan paperwork would not always be verified, making it easy for some buyers and mortgage brokers to provide false information. These risky loans were more likely to be offered to Black Americans, even if they had credit profiles comparable to white borrowers who received more favorable terms.

Existing homeowners thought they were refinancing to take advantage of lower mortgage rates, while new buyers thought they were qualifying for low mortgage rates (and low down payments); whereas, in fact, the lowered lending standards and higher-risk mortgages meant that household debt skyrocketed as people took on mortgages they could not afford. The loans were offered based on the assumption that home prices would continue to increase. When they did not, the economy came crashing down.

When home prices began to decline in 2006 after the collapse of the housing bubble, borrowers could not refinance their mortgages. Homeowners struggled to make skyrocketing mortgage payments, and as a result, many lost their homes. In turn, securities that had been backed by these same mortgages became almost worthless. Borrowers who were in over their head stopped making their monthly mortgage payments, while, at the same time, interest rates on adjustable-rate mortgages rose, leading to higher monthly payments. As a result of collapsing home values, banks could not recover the money lost on defaulted loans. When banks started to fail, panic increased. By 2007, the United States was officially in the midst of a mortgage crisis and the worst recession since the Great Depression. As Gretchen Morgenson writes for the *New York Times*, the supposed "democratization of credit" had actually turned "the American dream of

homeownership into a nightmare for many borrowers."
Now it was time for Hollywood to respond.

HOLLYWOOD

In the decade that followed the collapse of the housing
market, as owning a home became more difficult for
thousands of Americans, it also became more difficult
on-screen. Haunted home narratives began growing in
popularity. Whereas Hollywood only produced eight
haunted home films between 1980 and 1987, it produced
thirty-two films that included haunted homes between
2008 and 2016. It was not just that people realized homeownership was less accessible than they had been led
to believe. It was that homeownership became a literal
nightmare, and Hollywood, as it often does, tapped into
the zeitgeist.

Financial duress is a frequent plot point in many
haunted home narratives. After all, if your house is
haunted, the logical response would be to leave. However,
something prevents these homeowners from leaving, and
in the vast majority of cases, that reason is financial. People stay in bad housing situations because they cannot
afford to leave. People stay because all their money has
been invested in the aforementioned house, often pur-
chased at a steal for reasons that soon become obvious,

and so they cannot move. Haunted home narratives frequently beg the question: What is more terrifying, the supernatural or bankruptcy?

In an exchange from *Don't Be Afraid of the Dark* (Troy Nixey, 2010), that could just as easily be from any number of haunted home movies, Kim (Katie Holmes) tells her boyfriend, Alex (Guy Pearce), that they must leave the house. Alex does not take Kim seriously, protesting that every cent he has "is in that house," and Kim ends up dying as a result. In the episode "Murder House" of the television series *American Horror Story: Murder House* (FX, October 19, 2011), the first season of the horror anthology created by Ryan Murphy and Brad Falchuk, Vivien Harmon (Connie Britton) begs her husband, Ben Harmon (Dylan McDermott), to let them move. She knows the house they just bought is evil and will destroy them. He tells her that they cannot move because they cannot afford it. When she asks if they are broke, he says no, they have money, but it is "just tied up in this house," and they cannot get it back until they sell the house. In other words, the house owns *them*. In the episode "Halloween: Part 1" (FX, October 26, 2011), former residents of the house are shown via flashback also wanting to leave. However, Chad (Zachary Quinto) similarly tells his partner, Patrick (Teddy Sears), that they cannot leave because all their money "is in this house." They had planned to flip the house and "make a mint on it," but now they cannot "because the economy is in the shitter," as Chad explains. Like the Harmons, they are stuck.

The idea of profiting off a home purchase that then becomes a disaster is a central tenet in the Netflix television series *The Haunting of Hill House* (Mike Flanagan, 2018), in which the Crains buy an old home with plans to renovate and then resell it, just like Chad and Patrick. Initially, they are preoccupied by the money they will make by flipping, while the children are excited about the sheer size of the house. In the episode "Screaming Meemies," when the Crain family first arrives at Hill House, the children react with awe, describing the house as "insane," "a castle," and "bigger than anything" they have seen. The mother, Olivia (Carla Gugino), cautions her children that there is a lot of work to be done on the house but that once they are finished—and here Hugh (Henry Thomas) interrupts his wife to declare, "We're gonna be rich!" Olivia cautions her husband not to speak like that in front of the children, but Hugh's exuberance is unrelenting: "We're gonna be swimming in it!" he declares. By "it," of course, he means money. They forgot to take into account the supernatural.

Even when profit is not the main agenda, the status of homeownership always is. In *Amityville II: The Possession* (Damiano Damiani, 1982), the prequel to *The Amityville*

Horror (Stuart Rosenberg, 1979), Anthony Montelli (Burt Young); his wife, Delores (Rutanya Alda); and their four children move into the Amityville house, the suburban home of their dreams. The film opens with the children squealing with excitement over the new house, Anthony yanking the "for sale" sign out of the yard, and Delores declaring, "Look at it! It's ours! It's ours!" Seconds later, Delores and her elder daughter break into song: "Be it ever so humble, there's no place like home!" The mother then proclaims, "Home, sweet home," as she and her daughter walk toward the house. This early in the film, they are still delighted by their accomplishment of the American dream: they own a home.

Homeownership also promises new opportunities. In a flashback within the *American Horror Story: Murder House* episode "Afterbirth" (FX, December 21, 2011), Vivien tells her husband, Ben, that she is going to leave him and move to Florida after finding out about his recent affair with one of his students. He pleads with her to reconsider, to let the family have a "fresh start" in Los Angeles. When she refuses, saying that she cannot get past the affair, he shows her a photo of a house he wants to buy in Los Angeles. "It's right near Hancock Park, where all those big mansions from the '20s are. You always talked about how much you wanted a house like this," he says. She shakes her head, telling him that a house will not fix their problems, but he is more optimistic. He persists, showing her photos of the house's interiors, the "Tiffany lamps and everything," and raves about the office, so he "can see patients at home." He even jokes that maybe the house is haunted because the price is such a steal, but that seems a small price to pay for such a bargain. Ben reveals to Vivien that when he saw the listing for this particular house and envisioned living there, it felt like a movie: the entire family gathered around the fire, Violet reading, Vivien rocking a baby, while Ben stoked the fire. This house, he swears, will make their family whole again. "When I look at this place, for the first time I feel like there's hope," he says.

It is clear that Ben sees homeownership as a magical salve that will heal all their wounds, Tiffany lamps and an at-home office all that are needed to repair the damage done. The house—and, specifically, buying it—is the answer. Vivien eventually agrees. At first, the house brings with it the promise of happiness and personal fulfillment, an ideal of homeownership that, in this case, is a steal at far-below-market value.

The ideal of homeownership at a bargain is also an incentive in the first film of the Amityville franchise, *The Amityville Horror* (Stuart Rosenberg, 1979). A few minutes into the film, a real estate agent shows the Amityville house to George (James Brolin) and Kathy (Margot

Kidder) Lutz. After the couple find out about the house's past—in which the Montelli family was murdered—they withdraw to the attic to discuss the situation. Kathy tells her husband that she loves the house but that she is disturbed by the house's past. The sale price of $80,000 also feels enormous to her; she tells her husband that it "might as well be $800,000." However, her husband, who insists that "houses don't have memories," and therefore that the murders are not an issue, argues with her that the house is "worth $120,000 easy." He also points out that if the murders had not happened, there would be no way they could afford the house, which is all the encouragement Kathy needs. When the Lutz family moves in, we find out why buying the house had felt so unattainable for Kathy. "This is a big event in my family," she tells George. "We've always been a bunch of renters. It's the first time anyone has bought a house." It is almost understandable that an accomplishment like that would make one overlook a murder or two.

The allure of a bargain comes up over and over in haunted home narratives. The temptation of saving a few bucks also fuels the students in *American Poltergeist* (Michael Rutkowski, 2015) who move into a house off campus because it is "a sweet deal," as Michael (Luke Brandon Field) describes to his friends. When asked how he found the house, Michael responds, dismissing the question, "At $325 a month, including utilities, I mean, who cares?" The fact that the house is far from campus, comes with an eccentric homeowner, and has a sinister past all seem irrelevant when compared to the money that will be saved.

In *The Devil's Candy* (Sean Byrne, 2015), the artist Jesse Hellman (Ethan Embry); his wife, Astrid (Shiri Appleby); and their daughter, Zooey (Kiara Glasco), visit a potential future home, their jaws dropping during their initial tour over the home's size and condition. The real estate agent (Craig Nigh) explains that there were two deaths in the house, and Astrid nods, confirming that now she understands why "the price is so low." Unconcerned by her reservations, the real estate agent insists he has appointments lined up all day to see the house because "folks love a bargain." After all, as he goes on to explain, "it's not like Charlie Manson lived here." Astrid tells her husband that she finds the house's history to be creepy and does not want to move forward, but he disagrees, explaining that he finds the death of the couple who had lived there previously to be "really romantic" because the husband had killed himself after his wife died. Jesse mocks his wife's reservations, imitating the voice of a haunted spirit as he whispers, "Buy me." She relents, and they buy the house. Unsurprisingly, there is no happy-ever-after for this family in its new house. Jesse starts to hear voices, a possessed former resident of the home kidnaps Zooey, and things go from bad to worse.

In *Home* (Frank Lin, 2016), a couple purchase a house rumored to be haunted. They ignore the rumors, similarly focusing on the fact that they got "a good deal." This sounds as familiar as the evil events that begin to occur almost immediately upon moving in, and the couple soon regrets their purchase. What is unusual about the film is that the new homeowners are a same-sex couple (two women), a rarity for haunted home narratives, which are almost exclusively heteronormative. When asked about the choice to have the homeowners depicted as a same-sex couple, the producer, Jeff Lam, acknowledged that he and the director, Frank Lin, had planned to do so early on, before they had written a script. Lam explains that he and Lin wanted to portray a same-sex couple "in regular situations" and with "regular problems." Ironically, of course, the "regular problems" in this case include buying a home that is haunted. However, despite the unusual choice of making the homeowners a same-sex couple, it is worth noting that the two homeowners are absent for much of the drama, away on a business trip, leaving their older daughter, Carrie (Kerry Knuppe), and her boyfriend, Aaron (Aaron Hill), to feud with the evil spirits and protect the young stepsister, Tia (Alessandra Shelby

Farmer), thus, as usual, giving us a heterosexual couple as the force of "good."

Spiral (Kurtis David Harder, 2019) is the only haunted home narrative I was able to find with a same-sex couple (this time two men) at the center of the film. Interestingly, the film reflects many of the tropes of the traditional haunted home narrative, except that the characteristics normally attributed to the wife/mother manifest themselves, instead, in the more feminine of the two men. The couple are, like so many others, "house poor," struggling to pay their mortgage, excited to have left Chicago for a home that Malik (Jeffry Bowyer-Chapman) describes as a "palace" and as "paradise." Aaron (Ari Cohen), his partner, is so ready to embrace the suburban mind-set that he insists on leaving doors unlocked and gets irate when Malik installs a security system. Malik, reflecting "feminine intuition," is quick to realize that the house and the town are dangerous, pleading with Aaron to move, but Aaron, predictably enough, refuses, calling Malik paranoid and unstable. While all these elements are familiar enough, Malik simply playing the role of the wife/mother, there is one crucial difference. Not only are they unable to protect their daughter, Kayla (Jennifer Laporte), casting judgment on their parenting skills, but by the end of the film, all members of the family die. No one escapes. In haunted home narratives, the gays do not make it out alive.

Whether consciously or not, Hollywood has continued to propagate Lewis Mumford's depiction of suburbia with its uniform houses and uniform heteronormative families. Hollywood has also continued to reflect the glory of homeownership, the way that owning a house seems to fill so many of the requirements of successful adulthood, whatever the price.

2

THE SUBURBAN GOTHIC

Gothic fiction is generally associated with death, drama, and fear, often combining doomed romance narratives with dark aesthetics, gloomy mansions, evil villains, and/or the supernatural. Originating in England in the 1760s and 1770s, the genre was popularized by novels such as Horace Walpole's *The Castle of Otranto* (1764), Ann Radcliff's *The Mysteries of Udolpho* (1794), and Clara Reeve's *The Old English Baron* (1777). A typical tale might involve a combination of mistaken identities, unrequited love, crumbling castles, and persecuted heroines. By the 1800s, the genre met even greater success thanks to authors such as Edgar Allan Poe; Mary Shelley, whose book *Franken-stein* (1818) became a Gothic classic; and later that century, Bram Stoker, best known for his novel *Dracula* (1897), which made the undead synonymous with the Gothic.

The rise of Gothic fiction was also linked to a specific type of architecture associated with England in the second half of the eighteenth century. The "Gothic Revival" architectural style became even more popular during the early nineteenth century as architects aimed to revisit elements of Gothic architecture that had been popular in Europe during the Middle Ages. Architects used flying buttresses, ribbed vaults, stained glass, and sharply pointed spires to make cathedrals and churches taller, grander, and sturdier. These types of settings provided a key element for Gothic narratives, not only enhancing them with a sense of history and past tragedy but also heightening the foreboding atmosphere.

The American Gothic style, however, was forced to reinvent some of these key aspects and architectural styles due to a pronounced lack of castles and crumbling cathedrals in the United States. While ghosts and evil villains remained, dungeons would usually be replaced with caves or forests, and castles with southern plantations, crumbling or otherwise. However, when the location was less geographically specific, a specific subgenre of the American Gothic tradition was born: the "Suburban Gothic." Unlike with a traditional Gothic mansion, where ghosts and secrets seem destined to lie between the walls, suburbia offers an overdose of the ordinary—or at least it is supposed to. Unlike traditional Gothic narratives, where evil is expected to lurk among the ruins of an abandoned castle, suburbia should come complete with green lawns, friendly neighbors, and the promise of perfection.

After all, suburbia appeals precisely for its safety and security. Much as the director Tobe Hooper took advantage of in *Poltergeist* (1982), it was precisely this contrast between the banality of the suburban home and the horrors tucked inside that made these instances of horror or supernatural fantasy so wildly incongruous. As John Carpenter, known for his horror classics *Halloween* (1978), *The Thing* (1982), and *Christine* (1983), explains, "If horror can get there, it can get anywhere. . . . So a filmmaker, if he plays with that, can create fear. Lots of fear" (qtd. in Jones 64–65). Similarly, Stephen King explains that, in his ideal horror story, "the monster shouldn't be in a graveyard in decadent old Europe, but in the house down the street" ("Terror" 94).

Unsurprisingly, since one can be seen as a response to the other, the advent of the Suburban Gothic coincided with the frenetic suburban sprawl that followed World War II. Its origin is often traced to the work of Shirley Jackson, known for short stories such as "The Lottery" (1948) and the novel *The Haunting of Hill House* (1959), as well as the work of Richard Matheson, known for his novels *I Am Legend* (1954), *A Stir of Echoes* (1958), *Hell House* (1971), and *Bid Time Return* (1975). Jackson and Matheson took the vision of a suburban utopia depicted in shows like *Father Knows Best* (CBS, 1954–55; NBC, 1955–58; CBS, 1958–60), *Leave It to Beaver* (CBS, 1957–58;

ABC, 1958–63), and *The Donna Reed Show* (ABC, 1958–66) and fused it not only with current social anxieties but also with a distinctly Gothic atmosphere. Despite Matheson's reliance on the supernatural—*I Am Legend* features a vampire/zombie hybrid of sorts that later inspired George Romero's zombie classic *Night of the Living Dead* (1968)—both he and Jackson explored themes common to this new and potentially unsettling suburban life, such as isolation, depression, and repression. Horror narratives could not help but respond to the drastic changes taking place in US society, and for many, they became the perfect place in which to do so.

TRAUMA

Financial difficulties and white heteronormativity are only two troubling aspects of the US suburb. The suburbs had not been built merely as "a consolation prize" to veterans for having survived the war. Rather, part of the motivation had been "to pave over these soldiers' war experiences as quickly and completely as possible in order to assimilate them into civilian life and make them productive and reproductive members of society" (Knapp 201). In other words, suburban development was an attempt to sweep traumas of the past beneath perfectly manicured lawns.

In haunted home narratives, the repressed trauma is often emotional, made up of grief and loss, rather than a physical object, but it is still the past invading the present, the dead somehow coloring the living. As Robin Wood writes in his article "Return of the Repressed," the concept of the "terrible house" represents an extension of its inhabitants' personalities and, specifically, signifies the "dead weight of the past crushing the life of the younger generation, the future" (31). In turn, Barry Curtis writes in his book *Dark Places*, "'Ghosts' and the dark places where they dwell have served as powerful metaphors for persistent themes of loss, memory, retribution, and confrontation with unacknowledged and unresolved histories" (10). Ghosts represent anxieties over the potential porousness of the barrier between life and death, between past and present. In many haunted home narratives, the haunted house represents a specific point where the past refuses to stay in the past and, instead, threatens the present and the future.

Described by Freud as "repetition compulsion," a repeated theme in many haunted home narratives is the repetition of unresolved traumas until a proper resolution can be found. In the first episode of Mike Flanagan's *The Haunting of Hill House* (2018), a US television series created for Netflix and based on the 1959 novel of the same name by Shirley Jackson, Steven (Michiel

Huisman) explains to a woman that her house is not actually haunted. Rather, "the mind, it is a powerful thing,
ma'am, especially the grieving mind." She insists that
she saw her dead husband hanging from her ceiling, but
he persists: "If you push that stuff down, it comes out
at night. You couldn't help it." In other words, what you
repress will return. It is an unavoidable aspect of grief. He
explains that he has seen many ghosts, but not in the way
that she thinks. "A ghost can be a lot of things," he tells
her, "a memory, a daydream, a secret, grief, anger, guilt.
But in my experience, most times, they're just what we
want to see. . . . Most times a ghost is a wish."

More specifically, most times a ghost is a wish to resolve some sort of trauma. For example, in *Home* (Frank
Lin, 2016), Aaron (Aaron Hill) explains that usually,
when a person dies, "the spirit will realize what's happened and move on in the afterlife." However, some
spirits refuse to leave, even after they learn of their own
death, as a result of "some kind of emotional trauma." The
trauma creates a negative emotion that festers, Aaron
continues, "stripping the spirit of any humanity, leaving
only an angry entity." This angry entity will not leave until
the trauma is completely resolved.

Jessie (Sarah Snook) is in a brutal car accident at the
start of *Jessabelle* (Kevin Greutert, 2014). Badly injured,
she is forced to move in with her estranged father, Leon

(David Andrews), until she can walk again. Leon sets Jessie up in the bedroom that had belonged to Jessie's mother, Kate (Joelle Carter), who died shortly after Jessie was born. Not only is the bedroom metaphorically haunted by memories of Jessie's mother, but Jessie literally keeps seeing and hearing her mother, having discovered a box of videotapes her mother had recorded of herself shortly before she died. Jessie eventually discovers that Kate is not her actual mother and that Jessabelle, instead, had been Kate's daughter, fathered by a man named Moses. Furious about the affair, Leon had killed both Moses and Jessabelle, adopting Jessie so that no one would notice the missing baby. By the end of the movie, Jessie allows Jessabelle's spirit to move into her body, finally letting Jessabelle's tormented soul (and, by implication, Kate's soul, as well) find peace. Resolution comes only from a complete release of trauma, not from locking it deeper away. Once the trauma has been resolved, the spirit can find peace.

In *The Uninvited* (Lewis Allen, 1944), brother and sister Roderick (Ray Milland) and Pamela (Ruth Hussey) Fitzgerald are delighted to acquire Windward House, a beachside mansion, for a bargain price. Unfortunately, as is often the case with many of these "deals," the duo quickly discover that the house is haunted and had been the site of horrific family trauma. To make matters worse, local resident Stella (Gail Russell) is furious at her grand-father for selling the house because it is where her mother, Mary, had lived (and died). The Fitzgeralds, while investigating why their house is haunted, find out that Stella's father had had an affair with a Spanish gypsy named Carmel who became pregnant with his child. When Mary found out, she took Carmel to Paris under false pretenses. After Carmel's daughter was born, Mary stole the baby, named her Stella, and brought her back home, claiming that Stella was hers. Furious, Carmel stole Stella back and forced Mary off a cliff near Windward House. Not long after this confrontation, Carmel fell ill and died, her death hastened by the help of Miss Holloway (Cornelia Otis Skinner), eager to avenge her friend Mary's death. After the Fitzgeralds and Stella put all this together, Carmel's spirit is able to leave, relieved that her daughter finally knows the truth.

But resolution is not always complete, no matter how intense the wish to make it so. In *The Babadook* (Jennifer Kent, 2014), for example, the film's primary characters—a mother, Amelia Vanek (Essie Davis), and her son, Sam (Noah Wiseman)—are haunted by the unresolved grief and loss of her husband and his father, Oskar Vanek. Amelia still has not dealt with Oskar's death in a car accident six years prior, when he was killed driving her to the hospital to give birth to Sam. Every year, Sam's birthday provides an upsetting reminder of what also happened on that day. All of Oskar's possessions are still in the family's basement, where Sam plays with them, but Amelia cannot deal with them. Sam has no problem talking about his father's death, but Amelia refuses to talk about Oskar at all, even telling Sam, "I haven't been the same since your father died," as if that were the beginning and end of the story. Amelia is so repressed, in fact, that, for most of the film, she is not even capable of being loving to her son. She cringes from his touch. In an attempt to isolate herself from the trauma of Oskar's death, she isolates herself from everything and everyone.

Amelia and Sam's relationship worsens during the film, as Sam begins to insist that a monster—the Babadook—from one of his books is real. Both Amelia and Sam stop being able to sleep, roaches infest the house, and doors open and close by themselves. Amelia begins having disturbing hallucinations and grows crueler to Sam. Amelia's repeated attempts to destroy the Babadook book fail, as the book—and the monster—keeps returning. Near the end of the film, the Babadook pushes Amelia to revisit her husband's death, forcing her to expel her grief and trauma in a wave of fury. This release then allows her to dominate over the Babadook, trapping him in the basement, where he remains locked indefinitely. While this seems like resolution, the fact that she cannot get rid of him entirely reflects the fact that her trauma remains. It is just more repressed, locked further away.

HAUNTOLOGY

In the book *Hauntings: Psychoanalysis and Ghostly Transmissions*, Stephen Frosh discusses the concept of "hauntology," a term coined by the philosopher Jacques Derrida in his book *Spectres of Marx* in 1993. "Hauntology" describes the way the past can infringe on the present, the way the unseen haunts the seen. Derrida's original argument was that aspects of Marxism could (and would) linger over Western society long after the supposed death of communism. To those who were triumphant about the collapse of communism, to those who declared, "not only is it finished, but it did not take place, it was only a ghost," he warns, "a ghost never dies, it remains always to come and to come-back" (143).

Frosh takes the concept one step further, describing hauntology as a "precursor of post-colonial studies," in the sense that colonialism can be equated with "stealing, expunging, and overwriting the histories of oppressed groups." Despite whatever victories colonialists claim, the violence and trauma that occur as a result of their actions will inevitably haunt them (Frosh 54). This dynamic comes up explicitly in haunted home narratives that directly confront the cruelty faced by Native Americans at the hands of white Americans.

In the Netflix series *The Haunting of Hill House*, themes of unresolved grief and trauma are everywhere. The narrative cuts back and forth between multiple timelines, following the tragic and terrifying events that take place when the Crain family—Hugh, Olivia, and their children, Steven, Shirley, Theodora, Luke, and Nell—moves into Hill House and intercutting with present-day story lines exploring the long-term impact of those events while emphasizing how the past does not stay neatly in the past.

Trevor Macy, executive producer of *The Haunting of Hill House*, confirms that he sees a direct link between repressed trauma and hauntings. "A ghost is a memory of past trauma," he describes. "The things we carry with us emotionally in a very real sense determine what we are afraid of and show us who we are." When asked about the choice to tell the story of the Crain family in a nonlinear fashion, Macy explains that the primary purpose was to demonstrate the links between the characters' childhood trauma and their struggles as adults. "When you are exploring the roots of trauma," he says, "those are inseparable from childhood, and fear is largely inseparable from childhood. So you tell the story of these children and the way the ripples affect them as adults. In *Hill House*, the narrative of why the characters moved in there is an important fact for the audience to understand in order to relate to the characters as adults."

As the director of the *Hill House* series, Mike Flanagan, tells Mike Bloom of the *Hollywood Reporter*, "Each of us dug so deep into our own families and stories to try and inform the show. It had to be about the way every family is a haunted house, and everyone is wrestling with their ghosts from their own childhood and beyond— that echoes through decades. That's what I wanted to explore more of, more than the gothic horror and genre moments." Flanagan goes on to explain that "a ghost can be a premonition" or "an imagined manifestation of guilt." He intentionally wanted Hill House to feel like a collection of the "fractured psyches of the people who had been inside." Flanagan says that ghosts are boring, unless they are "directly tied to an experience, emotion, or something that's intrinsic to a character." After all, as he points out, "we're all haunted as people." For him, the primary point of interest behind the Hill House story is "the way every family is a haunted house, and everyone is wrestling with their ghosts from their own childhood and beyond" (qtd. in Bloom).

In the *Hill House* episode "Witness Marks," Hugh Crain asks his adult son Steven if he knows what "witness marks" are. Hugh goes on to explain that witness marks are scars—little marks, scrapes, lines, and divots—that act as an unofficial repair record when an official one does not exist. In this case, he is talking specifically about the antique clock at Hill House, but the same analogy can be used to describe past trauma. Humans do not come with a repair record. Instead, their life experience is etched within—scrapes, lines, and divots—and must be read by anyone seeking to understand who a person is.

Interestingly, Flanagan makes the residual effect of childhood trauma even more prevalent in his Netflix adaptation than it is in the original novel. In an article for *Vulture* about *The Haunting of Hill House*, Ruth Franklin observes that the Netflix adaptation "argues, brutally and constantly (also Freudianly), that we never truly get over childhood trauma; we just repress and repeat it." All five of the children reflect the repress/repeat cycle of repetition compulsion, "through depression, addiction, or other self-destructive behavior." In contrast, only Eleanor reflects this cycle of trauma and repression in the book.

A similar theme is featured in *It: Chapter Two* (Andrés Muschietti, 2019), which, while primarily taking place in the present day, features frequent flashbacks to 1989. The film emphasizes the connection between the two timelines by cutting back and forth between scenes of the characters as children and scenes of them as adults. Interestingly, once the adults have taken down the evil creature Pennywise (Bill Skarsgärd), who has haunted them since they were children, the scars on their hands that they collectively made to commemorate their bond—and their promise to come together if Pennywise returned—disappear, a physical reflection of the metaphorical scars healing within them. They have dealt with their childhood monsters—both the literal and the figurative ones. This evolution is reinforced when Pennywise tells the group that they have all grown up, while Pennywise, in contrast, regresses to babyhood.

Another kind of trauma that occurs in haunted home narratives is that which is tied to the physical walls of the house. Shirley Jackson had been interested in the work of the psychoanalyst and psychical researcher Nandor Fodor, known as an expert on poltergeists and other paranormal phenomena, as well as an associate of Sigmund Freud's. Fodor believed that ghosts and other related phenomena are actually external manifestations of repressed conflicts within the subconscious mind. Fodor also believed that homes could absorb the traumatic events that happened within them, which could cause a genuinely haunted house. The sudden appearance of a ghostly presence could be triggered, according to Fodor, by the activation of past negative energy by similar energy in the present.

In "Birth," the eleventh episode of *American Horror Story: Murder House* (FX, December 14, 2011), Constance hires the medium Billie Dean Howard (Sarah Paulson) to help banish the spirits of Chad (Zachary Quinto) and Patrick (Teddy Sears). As Billie walks around the Harmon family's home, she comments that she senses "so much pain, so much longing and regret, fear, sadness, guilt." When Constance asks if Billie can get rid of Chad and Patrick, Billie explains that "targeting a particular spirit is going to be difficult" since so many spirits fill the house. The only recourse is "to try and dislodge them from the paramagnetic grip" of the house. When Violet asks what that is, Billie replies, "The evil. It's a force just like any other, Violet: pure physics, real and powerful, created by events, events that unleash psychic energy into the environment, where it's absorbed—like the way a battery stores energy." Billie goes on to explain that this phenomenon is visible "in places like prisons or asylums" because "negative energy feeds on trauma and pain." There is a similar line in *The Conjuring 2* (James Wan, 2016), when Ed (Patrick Wilson) explains that "negative entities often feed off emotional distress. They like to kick you when you're down."

ISOLATION

Another negative aspect of suburbia is the isolation it fosters. The suburbs literally isolate—not only in separate houses with separate rooms but also in separate cars moving us to and from those houses. After all, this is the fundamental concept behind the suburban neighborhood as opposed to the urban one. Isolation provides the illusion of security, while the desire for security creates a need for isolation. As Hayden explains in her book *Redesigning the American Dream*, "for the first time in history, a civilization has created a utopian ideal based on the house rather than the city or the nation" (18). Lewis Mumford also emphasizes the isolationist tendencies of suburbia by describing its purpose specifically as allowing one "to withdraw like a monk and live like a prince" (299). One's "prince" status could be specifically determined by how much room individual members had from each other and by how much room existed between individual homes. If nothing else, this isolation was bound to have serious repercussions, both within the family itself and also between individual families. The isolationist nature of suburbia plays a key role not only in allowing the fear and terror to exist behind closed doors but also in perpetuating it, both on- and offscreen.

The standard narrative structure of a film or television show based around a haunted home inevitably features a series of supernatural events that gradually intensify, either psychologically or physically (or both). These events serve to isolate the family from people outside the house's walls, as well as to sow discord between family members. Individual members are either pitted against each other (on the basis of who believes what or where allegiances lie), or the family members are in conflict with those from outside who either do not believe or do not wish to help. The resolution comes only once the family has fled the house, destroyed the house, or both.

In *The Haunting of Hill House*, the characters are fundamentally isolated from each other, unable to communicate their own particular truth, and disbelieved when they attempt to do so. This refusal to believe, to acknowledge each other's reality, creates a sense of dissonance and separation. Macy explains that he and Flanagan were particularly drawn to the lies people tell each other in order to protect themselves, the evidence that they construct for themselves in order to talk themselves into or out of what they fear.

This refusal to acknowledge what is actually there is an underlying theme behind the entire series. The family seems (at least at first) to be close knit; however, the children and their parents repeatedly do not believe each other. For example, in the episode "A Twin Thing," young Nell (Violet McGraw) tells her twin, young Luke (Julian Hilliard), "Mommy and Daddy don't believe me, ever." When Nell sees "the bent-neck lady"—a disturbing ghost with a broken neck that will traumatize Nell for years until her death—her parents dismiss it as a nightmare. Much as husbands often do not believe their wives in these situation, parents frequently do not believe their children's warnings. In films as diverse as *The House by the Cemetery* (Lucio Fulci, 1981) and *A House Is Not a Home* (Christopher Ray, 2015), husbands do not believe wives, and parents do not believe children. Disbelief and denial are everywhere.

Steven (Michiel Huisman) is the oldest son in the Crain family. As an adult, he is a well-known author, most famous for writing about his family's experiences growing up in Hill House, all of which he dismisses due to mental illness. For instance, in the episode "Witness Marks," Steven describes his sister Nell as "delusional, depressed," his brother Luke as "an addict," his sister Shirley as "a control freak," and his sister Theo as "a clenched fist with hair." The whole family, in fact, "is on the brink of a breakdown," he declares, "seeing things that aren't there, hearing things that aren't there." He goes on to emphasize to his father that the issue is "not the house" but, rather, "something wrong with our goddamn brains," which is why he, specifically, has chosen not to have children. In the episode "Eulogy," adult Steven tells his brother Luke (Oliver Jackson-Cohen), "Hell, I've seen things this week, but it's not real. It's not." Steven warns Luke that if he, like their mother and their sister Nell, does not get his shit together and does not "stop talking like a fucking crazy person," he will "end up just like them" because the mental illness is in their genes: "it's a sickness."

In the episode "The Bent-Neck Lady," adult Nell (Victoria Pedretti) has a session with her therapist, Dr. Montague (Russ Tamblyn). Montague tells her that her underlying problem is that she has not confronted her past: "Every time we talk about your mother or your childhood or your symptoms . . . it always comes back to one thing: the house." The therapist does not understand how or why a house could have that much power. Even Nell resists acknowledging the supernatural forces at play, telling herself in the same episode that the house is "just a carcass in the woods," trying to use rational language to diminish the power the house has over her and her family. However, denial does not solve trauma, and so the repetition compulsion continues.

THE HOUSE

A haunted house, as depicted throughout the Halloween season, is traditionally described as multistoried and run down, with broken or boarded-up windows, isolated from its surroundings by physical distance, a menacing fence, and/or unkempt landscaping. In such classic fashion, Stephen King describes 29 Neibolt Street in his novel

It (1986) as "brooding and silent," with a "weedy yard" and "slumped porch" full of "empty beer cans, empty beer bottles, empty liquor bottles," along with "drifts of crumbled newspapers," "thick layers of old leaves," and "a smell like garbage." There are "boards nailed across its windows," and the house itself is far beyond the end of the sidewalk (314, 315). As ominous as the outside of the home is, the true danger lies within, and there is no renovation or cleaning crew that can eradicate the house's evil. It is for this reason that the house often needs to be destroyed by the end of the haunted home narrative in order for the evil forces to be defeated.

The most terrifying action usually takes place in extremes of the house, such as the basement or attic. The attic is the scene of horror in *Hereditary* (Ari Aster, 2018), *Burnt Offerings* (Dan Curtis, 1976), *The Disappointments Room* (D. J. Caruso, 2016), and *The Changeling* (Peter Medak, 1980), as well as where Sonny lurks as the demon takes over his body in *Amityville II: The Possession*, for instance. The basement (and the layers beneath it) is the scene of horror and evil, if not an actual portal to hell, in *The Amityville Horror* (Stuart Rosenberg, 1979), *The Conjuring* (James Wan, 2013), *The Innkeepers* (Ti West, 2011), *The House by the Cemetery* (Lucio Fulci, 1981), *The Babadook, Don't Be Afraid of the Dark* (Troy Nixey, 2010), *The Charnel House* (Craig Moss, 2016), *It: Chapter Two*, and

Amityville II, among many others. In *Amityville 4: The Evil Escapes* (Sandor Stern, 1989), the basement is a frequent source of horror, as well. While the possessed lamp operates from the attic, evil things repeatedly happen in the basement, including a chainsaw that turns itself on, a massive leak of questionable dark sludge, an unexplained amputated hand, and a plumber who is killed but whose body is never discovered. In *Don't Be Afraid of the Dark*, Kim (Katie Holmes) tells her boyfriend, Alex (Guy Pearce), that they must leave the house because "something terrible happened in that basement." When they do not leave, Kim ends up dying (in the basement). In *Amityville 6: It's About Time* (Tony Randel, 1992), teenage Lisa (Megan Ward), whose sexuality has intensified as a result of her proximity to the evil force, lures a boy down to the family basement and to his death, laughing as he is sucked into a burning pit of viscous fluid.

Physical location traps our characters as effectively as emotional trauma does, and one of the reasons for this is because the house is rarely ordinary, often taking on human characteristics. In Edgar Allan Poe's *The Fall of the House of Usher* (1839), for example, the protagonist describes "the vacant eye-like windows" and "the evidence of the sentience" to be found "in the gradual yet certain condensation of an atmosphere," as well as in the arrangement of the stones and decayed trees. The result of this sentience, Poe writes, can be found in the "silent yet importunate and terrible influence" that the house had on the Usher family (88, 96). Macy explains that Hill House is especially terrifying because "it can see the cracks in each person and flow into them."

Similarly, the synopsis of Susie Moloney's novel *The Dwelling* (2003) on the back cover of the book declares, "Three families buy 362 Belisle, but no one stays there for long. For this dream house has a mind and a heart of its own." Not only does the house have a heart and a mind, but it also has malevolent spirits. There is a comparable exchange in *The Changeling* when Minnie Huxley (Ruth Springford) from the local historical society tries to prevent John Russell (George C. Scott) from renting a particular home. "That house is not fit to live in," she warns him. "No one's been able to live in it. It doesn't want people." The "it" applies not merely to the structure itself but to whatever presence haunts those walls. John, further into the film, asks Claire Norman (Trish Van Devere), also from the historical society, "What is it in that house, Claire? What is it doing? Why is it trying to reach me?" Claire's reply is to tell John that he "must get out of that house." He does not.

The animated film *Monster House* (Gil Kenan, 2006) revolves around a sentient house that terrifies its entire neighborhood, attacking and eating neighborhood

children and even police officers (and their police car).
Unsurprisingly, adults refuse to believe the children who
witness these attacks. Forced to contend with the problem themselves, D.J. (voiced by Mitchel Musso), Chow-
der (Sam Lerner), and Jenny (Spencer Locke) discover
that the house is actually a fusion of a human soul with
a manmade structure and that the only way to kill it is by
attacking its heart. In their attempt to destroy the house,
the children also manage to free the ghost trapped within
its walls, which then releases all those who had previously
been eaten—trauma resolved!

In Shirley Jackson's novel *The Haunting of Hill House*,
the house is also described as a sentient being, not just
replete with atmosphere but also with personality and
character. The house is actually evil and can even be seen
as the antagonist in the story. As Elena Nicolaou writes,
"Hill House is a malevolent entity which singles out its
inhabitants and bullies them with strange events—blood
oozes out of walls, random messages appear. But there
are no ghosts in Jackson's book. The house can't physically harm anyone. It can, however, drive a person mad."
The novel begins with a description of Hill House as "not
sane," standing "by itself against its hills, holding darkness
within" (Jackson 8). When Eleanor first sees the house,
she describes it as "vile" and "diseased" (25). Her initial
instinct is to get away at once, but, of course, she does not.

Later in the book, Jackson writes, "No human eye can isolate the unhappy coincidence of line and place which suggests evil in the face of a house, and yet somehow a manic juxtaposition, a badly turned angle, some chance meeting of roof and sky, turned Hill House into a place of despair, more frightening because the face of Hill House seemed awake, with a watchfulness from the blank windows and a touch of glee in the eyebrow of a cornice" (26). She goes on to write that the house seems to "have formed itself, flying together into its own powerful pattern, . . . fitting itself into its own construction of lines and angles" (26). And this construction appears deliberately designed to destabilize any humans unlucky to walk through its doors. As Eleanor observes, the house has "an unbelievably faulty design which left it chillingly wrong in all its dimensions, so that the walls seemed always in one direction a fraction longer than the eye could endure, and in another direction a fraction less than the barest possible tolerable length" (29).

In Jackson's original version of the tale, Dr. John Montague, who specializes in the paranormal, wants to find scientific evidence to prove the existence of the supernatural. He rents Hill House, which features a dark and violent history and is generally considered to be haunted. Montague organizes a small group, including Eleanor

Vance, a shy and introverted young woman with psychic abilities who has devoted much of her life to caring for a sick mother; Theodora, an outgoing, flirtatious, and confident artist and clairvoyant; and Luke Sanderson, the heir to Hill House. The house's caretakers—Mr. and Mrs. Dudley—are around during the daytime but refuse to stay at the house past dark.

As the doctor shows his guests around the home, he points out the extreme difficulty they have finding their way around, comparing Hill House to the Winchester House in California. He attributes much of this to strategy on the part of Hugh Crain, who designed and built Hill House and who intentionally made every angle "slightly wrong" (Jackson 67, 68). The doctor explains to the others that the house is "a masterpiece of architectural misdirection" and that "the result of all these tiny aberrations of measurement adds up to a fairly large distortion in the house as a whole" (68). Luke adds that these architectural abnormalities could cause "a slight loss of balance" among residents of the home (69). While the doctor credits Hugh Crain with creating a home that deliberately destabilizes, it is not clear whether that is merely Montague's theory. After all, if the house "formed itself," perhaps Crain had no say in the matter? Even Eleanor perceives that "the builders of the house had given up any attempt at style—probably after realizing what the house was going to be, whether they chose it or not" (27–28).

Jackson never clarifies if the house is actually evil, if it is possessed by the ghosts of the people murdered there, or if the horrific visions are in the minds of Montague's team. However, as Montague speculates, "The evil is the house itself, I think. It has enchained and destroyed its people and their lives, it is a place of contained ill will" (54). At the same time, the ambiguity also makes it clear that there is a psychological component that makes certain people more vulnerable than others. Sarah Lotz argues that "the best haunted house narratives are never just about the dead—they're about the living and the psychological. In *Hill House*, the real horror comes from the tragedy that Eleanor thinks she is escaping her stultifying family situation, but can't escape her own mind" (qtd. in Flood). Or, as Mike Flanagan puts it, "Eleanor in the novel has walled herself off from society; she's so sheltered and has never really left home. She goes from this completely contained and insular existence to what she perceives as the expansive world around her. And it's just another house; it's another box" (qtd. in Bloom).

The Netflix adaptation makes clear that the sentient qualities of the house are also to blame for the family's deterioration. Andrew Whalen writes that "matriarch Olivia Crain (Carla Gugino) designs the perfect house for her family, but finds her blueprints corrupted by Hill House's evil influence." This corruption transforms the home "from a positive vision of nurturing and fellowship into a psychic fortress." In the episode "Two Storms," an older Hugh Crain (Timothy Hutton) tries to convince his son Steven that the problems in the Crain family are not due to mental illness but rather to the house itself. In *American Horror Story: Murder House*, in the episode "Halloween: Part 1" (FX, October 26, 2011), Chad tells Vivien that her family should move: "We know it, you know it, and the house knows it." In the episode "Piggy Piggy" (FX, November 9, 2011), Constance tells Violet, "I questioned my sanity when I first found out. But this house, this house will make you a believer. You see, Violet, we were living here when Tate lost his way. And I believe that the house drove him to it."

Similarly, in Stephen King's novel *The Shining* (1977), the Overlook Hotel is the source of the evil, rather than the character of Jack Torrance. One of the reasons King was critical of Stanley Kubrick's film adaptation (1980) is that King felt Kubrick had diminished the role of the hotel, chalking up most of the evil to Jack, instead. Interestingly, the film's sequel, *Doctor Sleep* (Mike Flanagan, 2019), also based on a book by King, emphasizes the hotel *both* as a sentient being *and* as a source of evil, which is why the hotel must be burned down at the film's end. As

Abra Stone (Kyliegh Curran) explains, "The fire spread fast, destroying the hotel, purifying it. I could almost hear it screaming. I could hear it dying."

This notion of a house as a sentient being shows up over and over. In *The Legend of Hell House* (John Hough, 1973), a British horror film based on Richard Matheson's novel *Hell House* (1971), the wealthy and eccentric Mr. Deutsch hires a group of researchers—a physicist, the physicist's wife, and two mediums—to investigate the Belasco House, widely considered to be haunted by the ghosts of those who had been tortured and killed by its former owner, Emeric Belasco. The dying Mr. Deutsch wants the researchers to investigate whether there is life after death. In this respect, the plot is very similar to that of Jackson's novel *The Haunting of Hill House*, which had been inspired by a group of nineteenth-century researchers who had moved into a house considered to be haunted in order to prove whether the house was actually haunted. Another similarity between *The Legend of Hell House* and *The Haunting of Hill House* is that the Belasco House is also considered to be a sentient being. When the researchers arrive at the Belasco House, Florence Tanner (Pamela Franklin), a mental medium, declares with trepidation in her voice, "This house . . . it knows we're here." A few minutes later, Benjamin Fischer (Roddy McDowall), a physical medium, the only known survivor of a previous research stay at the house, recounts how the house tried to kill him and "almost succeeded."

In *House on Haunted Hill* (William Malone, 1999), a remake of the 1959 film of the same title directed by William Castle, the familiar premise is that a group of strangers have been promised $1 million if they survive a night at the eponymous house. The owner of the building, Watson Pritchett (Chris Kattan), who grew up in it, is convinced not only that the house is haunted but specifically that "it's alive." Stephen Price (Geoffrey Rush), like the others in the group, disregards Pritchett's warnings until it is too late, at which point, with ten minutes left in the movie, Price concedes that Pritchett was right and the house *is* alive. Remarkably, the movie features a Black actor, Taye Diggs, in the role of Eddie. What is even more remarkable is that Eddie is one of only two people to survive the night. Quite often, Black characters are the first to die in horror movies.

The television miniseries *Rose Red* (ABC, 2002) also features a house imbued with human characteristics. Scripted by Stephen King and loosely based on Robert Wise's film *The Haunting* (1963), which was, in turn, based on Jackson's novel *The Haunting of Hill House*, the miniseries borrowed heavily from the history of the real Winchester Mystery House in San Jose, California. Of particular significance to *Rose Red* are the claims that ghosts of people killed with Winchester rifles haunt the house, as well as the building's curious architectural style. An enormous building, the Winchester House was famously built without a master plan. Sarah Winchester, the chief resident and widow of the firearms tycoon William Winchester, continued to add rooms and wings to the building through to her death, leading to many irregularities and a general maze-like nature, compounded by doors and stairs that do not actually lead anywhere, as well as windows that merely look out into other rooms. Similarly, in Jackson's novel, the house disorients as a result of countless architectural irregularities.

While *Rose Red* was initially pitched as a feature film by King to Steven Spielberg, the two could not agree on the right mix of action and horror, so they went their separate ways; with Spielberg producing the remake of *The Haunting* directed by Jan de Bont and released in 1999 and King turning his project into a miniseries. The basic premise behind the miniseries is that Dr. Joyce Reardon (Nancy Travis), a psychology professor at the local college, is fascinated by the paranormal and determined to prove that it exists. Her plan is to bring a team of psychics to the supposedly haunted Rose Red mansion (the sprawling home inspired by the Winchester House) and to document the events that she is certain will transpire, providing her with the irrefutable scientific proof that she desperately desires. Referencing Jackson right off the bat, Reardon introduces Rose Red by saying, "Shirley Jackson was right. Some houses are born bad."

The third and final episode of the miniseries opens with a voice-over by Reardon speaking over various shots of the Rose Red mansion. "A house is a place of shelter," she says. "It's the body we put on over our bodies. As our bodies grow old, so do our houses. As our bodies may sicken, so do our houses sicken." As she says these last words, we can see cracks spreading throughout the house. "And what of madness?" she goes on to ask. "If mad people live within, doesn't this madness creep into the rooms and walls and corridors, the very boards?" We see more shots of the house, of dead bodies within it, of overgrown shrubbery and neglect outside it. "Isn't that a large part of what we mean when we say a place is unquiet, festered up with spirits? We say haunted, but we mean the house has gone insane."

Much as horror narratives provide an allegorical outlet for exploring our fears and anxieties about poorly repressed grief and trauma, the Suburban Gothic—with the suburban home as its centerpiece—makes repeated attempts to portray the home as we are afraid it might be: the locus of debt, dysfunction, and death. A close examination of the home, and everything that hides within, exposes the rot at the heart of suburbia, the ugliness behind the misogyny, oppression, and racism barely concealed behind the white picket fence.

3

GENDER, HORROR, AND THE HOME

As the suburbs grew in size and popularity throughout the twentieth century, the family took center stage in American life. Couples married early and had children shortly thereafter, filling up the multiple bedrooms in their new homes. Fewer women considered higher education as gender roles emphasized a sharp split between men (who pursued careers) and women (who pursued children). Despite efforts to sell the suburban dream as empowering for wives and mothers—film, television, magazines, and advertising all pitched the home as a place for women to attain power, control, and personal fulfillment—the restrictive solitude, as well as other aspects of gender dictated by suburban life, had far reaching (and negative) repercussions. Dolores Hayden, in her book *Redesigning the American Dream*, argues that "women's status is lowest in societies where women are most separated from public life. And in the United States the suburban home is the single most important way of separating women" (50).

That solitude grew. As men's commutes got longer and longer (since families were forced to move farther from city centers as housing prices rose), women were left without adult companionship for hours at a time. Grady Hendrix argues that Shirley Jackson's *The Haunting of Hill House* is primarily about this loneliness, a feeling common to Jackson in her real life. In an article for *The Guardian*, Alison Flood references Hendrix, pointing out that Jackson herself felt that one of the pivotal moments in *Hill House* was when Eleanor, thinking that she is holding Theo's hand, suddenly realizes that Theo is nowhere nearby. "Whose hand was I holding?" Eleanor cries out. Flood quotes Hendrix describing Jackson, "For a woman constantly criticized by her mother, alienated by her husband, and isolated by her neighbors, the worst answer of all is: 'No one's.'" Many women had no one to hold their hand during the 1950s.

Published in 1963, Betty Friedan's book *The Feminine Mystique* explores how unfulfilling life as a housewife could be, even though persistent messaging told women that all they needed to be happy was a husband, a home, and a couple of children. A different kind of messaging applied to the husband, who was expected to be confident and aggressive, capable with finances and home repair.

He should feel at home in the garage or in the boardroom, with the barbeque or the power tools, while the wife maintained the rest of the house—or so the suburbs dictated. By the 1970s, it may have become more common for each parent to have their own career, but women were still expected to be the caretakers and men the primary breadwinners, in many ways causing even more stress. These gender binaries not only propagated isolation but also made it more likely for aggressive males to dominate their submissive partners physically and emotionally. These binaries also made it difficult for either gender to step outside its assigned categories.

DOMESTIC VIOLENCE

A significant theme of the Suburban Gothic tradition is that, unlike with most conventional horror narratives, in which the external threat could be a vampire, an alien, or a serial killer, danger often comes from within: if not from within the family, then from within the home itself. For example, in *Malicious* (Michael Winnick, 2018), David (Ben VanderMey) explains to Lisa (Bojana Novakovic) and Adam (Josh Stewart)—a married couple that relocates to a new house in a new town—that homes are usually left unlocked in their town. Adam asks if that is safe, and David replies that, in his experience, "most people's problems happen behind closed doors." The threat is already inside.

This theme appears to be a direct response to a specific aspect of suburbia: the chilling realization that, for many women and children, the home is the most dangerous place. Contrary to the stereotypical notion that a home is one's castle—and if not a castle, then at least a fortress—the home is actually where women are most likely to be attacked. In an article titled "30 Domestic Violence Statistics That Remind Us It's an Epidemic," Alanna Vagianos compares the number of troops killed in Afghanistan and Iraq between 2001 and 2012 to the number of American women who were murdered by current or former male partners during that time: 6,488 to 11,766.

Some other horrifying statistics Vagianos mentions that paint a grim portrayal of domestic violence in the United States are that 85 percent of domestic violence victims are women; three women are murdered every day by a current or former male partner; the number of women who have experienced violence from a partner at least once in their lifetime is 38,028,000, with 4,774,000 women experiencing physical violence by an intimate partner every year; one in four women are victims of severe violence by an intimate partner in their lifetimes; and a woman is beaten every nine seconds. When the violence happens indoors, within the supposed safety of our walls, the attack is doubly violating because then nowhere is safe.

In haunted home narratives, women are frequently the recipients of violence, either from actual humans or from ghosts. In *The Entity* (Sidney J. Furie, 1982), based on the 1978 novel by Frank De Felitta, Barbara Hershey plays a woman, Carla Moran, who is repeatedly raped in her home by someone or something she cannot see. Despite the bruises on her body, doctors refuse to believe her, a chilling reflection of how many real-life rape accusations are disbelieved. Carla cannot afford to move, and so the violence continues. Her therapist, thinking she is on the verge (if not actually in the middle) of a nervous breakdown, wants Carla to commit herself. The therapist even explicitly tells Carla that when people see demons, it is only "a way of expressing what was frightening to them," rather than an actual physical threat. When Carla attempts to find help by turning to experts in the paranormal, the therapist tries to prevent her, actively wanting to block any attempt to acknowledge that maybe her threat is real.

The trope of being raped by a ghost also shows up in *The Legend of Hell House* (John Hough, 1973), based on the 1971 novel by Richard Matheson. In this film, a physicist and several mediums are hired to investigate possible paranormal activity in the Belasco House. While the mediums are more open-minded, the physicist, of course, refuses to believe in the supernatural. The evil spirit haunting the house rapes Florence Tanner (Pamela Franklin), one of the two mediums. As if this were not bad enough, a falling crucifix kills her soon after—perhaps representing death by the patriarchy?

A satire of many horror-film tropes, *Scary Movie 2* (Keenen Ivory Wayans, 2001) also includes a rape by a ghost, only in this case, Alex (Tori Spelling) enjoys it. In the satire *A Haunted House* (Michael Tiddes, 2013), one of the rare haunted home narratives featuring a Black cast, a demon rapes Kisha (Essence Atkins), the female lead. Like Alex, Kisha enjoys it and actively tries to seduce the demon to make it happen again. While there is some humor value to poking fun at a predictable trope— however unfunny rape actually is—the film also portrays Malcolm (Marlon Wayans), the male protagonist, being raped by the ghost. In marked contrast, this scene is brutal and uncomfortable to watch, as is Malcolm's shame following the incident.

In *The Amityville Horror* (Stuart Rosenberg, 1979), George Lutz (James Brolin) becomes increasingly menacing to his wife, Kathy (Margot Kidder), and her children. A half hour into the movie, he is chopping wood intensely—enough wood to "heat the whole South Shore," or so his wife tells him. Kathy comes over to say hello and ask for help with the groceries. "Don't ever do that," he barks at her, a scary look in his eye. As the film progresses, he becomes increasingly obsessed with chopping wood and keeping the living-room fire going, sharpening his axe with growing malevolence. An hour into the movie, his mood getting darker, he shouts at Kathy that her kids "need some goddamn discipline." When his coworker comes over to get George to sign the payroll checks since George has not come into work, George does not stop sharpening his axe until he gets so angry that he lifts his axe in anger, throwing it into a nearby tree.

The tension grows as George becomes increasingly stressed about being able to pay the mortgage, much less care for his wife and her three children. "Oh, mother of God, I'm coming apart," he shouts, tearing at his hair, his eyes bloodshot. When Kathy runs to care of him, he growls at her to stop nagging him. She suggests that the family leave, that they pack up their things and go, but he does not even look at her, preoccupied with putting more wood on the fire. When she implores him to stop with the fire and listen to her, he stands up, full of rage. "We're not going anywhere," he shouts at her. "You're the one that wanted a house. This is it, so just shut up!" He, of course, neglects to mention that he had been the one who convinced her that they should buy the place. When she spits out the words, "You bastard," he slaps her so hard that she almost falls over.

Shortly thereafter, during the climax of the film, George chases after his wife and her kids with his freshly sharpened axe. Just as the character of Jack Torrance (Jack Nicholson) does in *The Shining* (Stanley Kubrick, 1980), George walks through the house, blood dripping from the walls and stairs. He begins to break down the children's bedroom door with his axe, but then Kathy runs over and grabs him, trying to stop him. He knocks her to the floor and swings the axe down, as if to slice her open. He narrowly misses, and the shock of almost killing his wife makes him snap out of his trance. As the house begins to tremble and shake, George comes to his senses, helping his family escape.

In *Amityville II: The Possession* (Damiano Damiani, 1982), Anthony Montelli (Burt Young) is overbearing and abusive to both his wife, Delores (Rutanya Alda), and their four children. Seconds into the film, one of the children, Patricia (Diane Franklin), declares, "Daddy's such a creep." In Anthony's first exchange with his teenage son, Sonny (Jack Magner), Anthony warns Sonny that he is not "too big for a whipping," to which Sonny replies, "Yeah, I know. You proved that to me." Anthony ends the discussion by telling his son to learn how to take orders and demanding a "yes, sir" in response. In a subsequent scene, Anthony whips the two younger children with a belt. When Delores tries to stop him, he pushes her to the floor and chases after the children with the belt in his hand. When she again tries to stop him, he begins to beat her. The screams wake up the older children, who come downstairs to protect their mother. Sonny grabs his father's gun and points it at Anthony's head. Delores takes the gun away from a shaking Sonny and whispers at no one in particular, "Oh, my God, what's happening to us?"

When the evil presence in the house possesses Sonny, it feels as if Sonny is mimicking his father's violent tendencies. In what could easily be considered statutory rape, Sonny seduces his sister Patricia, much as his father had raped his mother. In this movie, as in so many others, the men (regardless of whether they are actually possessed or just cruel) dominate the women. Not only did the original cut of the film show Sonny and Patricia having sex, but it also showed Anthony anally raping Delores. Both scenes were cut from the final version of the film due to bad reactions during test screenings. However, while the actual sex scene between Sonny and Patricia was cut, the act is still heavily implied. We see them flirting with each other, we see her taking off her clothes, and we see her confessing the act to her family's priest.

As if a reference to the cycle of abuse, the abused continues to be the abuser. It is not long before Sonny—his face white and deformed—grabs a shotgun and begins to kill his family. First, Sonny shoots his father, then his mother, before slowly killing off his siblings, one at a time. Patricia desperately tries to escape, but because all the windows are nailed shut and will not break, she is trapped in the house, the home once again the most dangerous place for a woman. In a particularly torturous series of events, she is the last one shot. While this level of violence is new to the Montelli family, it is clear that a certain level of violence had always existed.

Horror narratives can expose this reality without any subterfuge. Mike Flanagan, director of the Netflix adaptation of *The Haunting of Hill House* (2018), observes, "In horror, in particular, the way people behave in their families is different than the way they behave out in the world. It strips away all the pretext" (qtd. in Bloom). For instance, in *The Boy* (William Brent Bell, 2016), Greta (Lauren Cohan) accepts a job as a nanny in the United Kingdom for the Heelshire family, partly to get farther away from her abusive ex-boyfriend, Cole (Ben Robson). The film implies that, because of a miscarriage Greta suffered as a result of one of Cole's beatings, she is especially attached to her latest ward, a porcelain doll named Brahms that appears to contain the spirit of the Heelshire family's dead child. While her difficulty leaving is exacerbated by her unresolved maternal issues, her problematic relationships with Cole and Brahms reinforce the difficulty that Greta has in getting away from controlling male figures.

Cole does track down Greta, planning to force her to move back home. When Brahms (the doll) intervenes, Cole breaks the doll. This triggers the actual Brahms (James Russell) to emerge from behind the wall, revealing the secret room where he has been living for years. Brahms kills Cole before turning his wrath on Greta and her friend Malcolm (Rupert Evans). In order to rescue Malcolm, Greta must stab Brahms as he tries to choke her. She finally manages to escape, leaving not one but two abusive relationships behind.

There are many more examples of domestic abuse in haunted home narratives. Single mom Courtney Collins (Shannyn Sossamon) unknowingly moves herself and her two children into a haunted house because she is hiding from an abusive husband in *Sinister 2* (2015). She goes from one source of danger to another, innocently thinking that the isolation of the new house and property will save her, rather than realizing that the truth is quite the opposite.

In *The Charnel House* (Craig Moss, 2016), father Alex becomes increasingly violent and aggressive. It appears as if evil forces in his apartment building are turning him into a threat against his family, so much so that he asks a neighbor to take his daughter, Mia (Makenzie Moss), away, knowing that he cannot be trusted to be alone with her. Alex continues to be violent and increasingly psychotic throughout the film, even stabbing one of his neighbors to death. Again echoing Jack Torrance in *The Shining*, Alex roams the hallways, a large glittering and bloody knife in his hand, calling for his daughter. When he finds his wife, Charlotte (Nadine Velazquez), he walks menacingly toward her, knife in hand. When she tells him that he is scaring her, he replies by asking her what she is scared of, continuing to bear down on her, knife in hand. When she tells him that she knows about his father and the murders he committed, Alex just says, "You're not going to take her away," and keeps walking toward her with the knife. Charlotte escapes and runs off to look for Mia. When she finds Mia, the first thing Mia says to her mother is, "Daddy's coming. Daddy's going to hurt us."

If women in haunted home narratives are not clearly raped, beaten, and/or killed, they repeatedly have bruises with inexplicable sources, as in *The Entity*. For instance, unexplained bruises appear over and over on the body of the mother, Carolyn (Lily Taylor), in *The Conjuring* (James Wan, 2013), and the evil spirit eventually drags her to the cellar and attacks her. In *I Am the Pretty Thing That Lives in the House* (Osgood Perkins, 2016), live-in nurse Lily Saylor (Ruth Wilson) discovers that a previous resident of the house had beaten his wife to death and hidden her body behind a wall. In turn, the ghost of the dead woman scares Lily, and she dies of a heart attack.

David Church, in his article "Return of the Return of the Repressed: Notes on the American Horror Film 1991–2006," writes that the repeated violence against women in these narratives can be viewed as part of a "wider remasculinization throughout American cinema that can be read as a backlash against feminism (and other liberation movements)" (19). Women may gain more and more freedom and independence offscreen, but at least in horror films, they can be put back in their place. And if the bruises come at the hands of a supernatural demon or as a result of evil forces, so that men can remain blameless, so much the better.

"CRAZY" WOMEN

Horror movies, and haunted home narratives in particular, tend to exaggerate the gender binary. Women are frequently seen as more vulnerable, intuitive, emotional, and prone to mental collapse. While this increased sensitivity makes them more aware, both emotionally and physically, of the hauntings, it also makes them more likely to be dismissed as crazy. When a woman tells people what she is experiencing, even if she has the bruises to show for it, they often refuse to believe her. In turn, men are seen as more aggressive, rational, and pragmatic—reluctant to believe in anything that does not follow rules of science or logic. Often traveling or working, men are more likely to be absent parents in haunted home narratives, emotionally as well as physically. When they are involved in child care, it is either to point out how bad they are at it or that they have to do it to compensate for how bad their partner is at it.

One way to understand this contrast is by noticing how many times men accuse women of being hysterical or crazy, a phenomenon that is far from new. In the episode "Rubber Man" of the television series *American Horror Story: Murder House* (FX, November 23, 2011), Moira O'Hara (Frances Conroy) tells Vivien Harmon (Connie Britton), "Since the beginning of time, men find excuses to lock women away. They make up diseases, like hysteria." She goes on to emphasize that things are no better today because "men are still inventing ways to drive women over the edge." Moira emphasizes that Vivien is "not crazy" and that "the house is possessed," despite the fact that Vivien's husband refuses to believe her. Validated, Vivien rushes to tell her daughter, Violet (Taissa Farmiga), that they are leaving the house immediately. The two of them pack their bags and head for the car. As they put on their seatbelts, Vivien tells Violet that they do not "have to be prisoners to this house anymore," the implication being that her husband was keeping them prisoner. Unfortunately, malevolent spirits are in the back seat of the car, forcing Vivien and Violet to flee back inside the house. When Vivien's husband, Dr. Ben Harmon (Dylan McDermott), finds out about the attempted escape, he berates her, telling her that he will not allow her to leave with Violet or the babies with which she is pregnant. Vivien insists that the spirits had been in the car, but Ben refuses to believe Vivien or his daughter.

In *The Forgotten* (Joseph Ruben, 2004), Telly (Julianne Moore) desperately searches for her missing son, a son everyone else tells her never existed. Dr. Jack Munce (Gary Sinise) tells her that it is totally normal for people to invent alternate lives with imagined friends, family, and children. The implication is not that people make things up but that *women* "make things up." This is also nothing new. In Greek mythology, Apollo gave Cassandra the gift of prophecy. Angry that she was not properly grateful, he then cursed her, making sure that no one would believe any of her prophecies, however accurate. While in *The Forgotten* there is a sense of triumph when Telly is shown to have been right all along, this sense of triumph rarely exists in haunted home narratives. Instead, the film's ending is usually colored by the fact that family members have lost their lives and the dream home has become a nightmare. By the time the woman is shown to be right, it is often too late for triumph.

In *Visions* (Kevin Greutert, 2016), Eveleigh (Isla Fisher) and David Maddox (Anson Mount) move into a new house, trying to put behind them a tragic car accident one year earlier in which Eveleigh accidentally killed a child—an event that has clearly cursed her, because what kind of woman kills a child? Eveleigh, now pregnant, begins to have horrifying visions. In this case, her heightened senses are dismissed by everyone around her as "mommy sense," also known as "too many hormones." Only Sadie (Gillian Jacobs), one of Eveleigh's friends, believes her, arguing that Eveleigh's protective instincts "are at an all-time high," so if something evil *had* happened in the house, she would be in a unique position to sense what others could not. While another woman can recognize this ability, none of the men do.

To make matters worse, Eveleigh's (male) doctor insists that she resume taking antidepressants, arguing that they will stop the visions. This suggestion is made in many of these narratives, including *The House by the Cemetery* (Lucio Fulci, 1981) and *The Disappointments Room* (D. J. Caruso, 2016). Unfortunately for poor Eveleigh, just like with the other women, the visions continue since they are not due to stress or depression. She pleads with her husband to let them leave the house, but he refuses, saying that she is just being hysterical and insisting that they have "sunk everything" they have into the house— once again financial stress keeps them there. By the end of the film, it is revealed that Eveleigh's instincts, much like Vivien's and Telly's, had been correct, but it is too late.

In *Something Evil*, a 1972 made-for-television horror film directed by Steven Spielberg and inspired by William Peter Blatty's novel *The Exorcist*, the Worden family— Marjorie (Sandy Dennis), Paul (Darren McGavin), and their two children—move into their dream house. Marjorie quickly realizes that there are "many strange things" in the house, telling her husband that "something or someone is trying to possess" her and her son. He refuses to take her seriously, telling her she is crazy. He makes jokes and ignores her pleas, reminding her that she is the one who wanted to move to this house. He tells her that all their money is in the house and that they cannot afford to leave. To make matters worse, Paul is frequently absent, as a result of his long commute and business trips, leaving Marjorie to deal with the evil alone.

In *The Haunted* (1991), a made-for-television movie directed by Robert Mandel, Jack (Jeffrey DeMunn) refuses to believe his wife, Janet (Sally Kirkland), that their new home is haunted. He dismisses her fears as stress related, calling her crazy. The local priest also dismisses Janet, telling the couple that they just need marriage counseling. Janet begs her husband to let them move, but he refuses, since, unsurprisingly, all their money is tied up in the house. When she tries to convince him to bring in demonologists, he also refuses, asking her what the neighbors would say. Even Father Kent (Jake Jacobs) will not believe her. Instead, he tells her, "Janet, I don't think you're lying. Sometimes we think we see things, horrible things, when we're just not feeling very special in this world." She begs him not to leave, crying that she needs his help to protect her and her children, but he leaves anyway, forcing her to face the problem on her own.

Perhaps it is appropriate that the woman is often left to face the problem, since, after all, a haunted home is a domestic matter. Unlike traditional narratives in which the male hero has to vanquish the threat, in these stories, the wife/mother is often the only hope. It falls on her to protect her family and get rid of the evil spirits. As often happens on- and offscreen, it falls on her to clean up the house, literally and metaphorically. In the first episode of *American Horror Story: Murder House* (FX, October 5, 2011), Vivien asks Moira if she ever gets tired "of cleaning up other people's messes." Moira says no, that they are women and it is what they do. This is absolutely what they do in these narratives, time and time again.

BAD MOMS AND DISTANT DADS

Women are not always portrayed as good parents in haunted home narratives. Even if they do manage to save their children, both women and men are usually depicted as deeply flawed parental figures. Much as the Suburban Gothic explores anxieties about suburban living, such as the realization that the home can actually be the most dangerous place for its inhabitants, it also provides an allegorical outlet for another suburban-related fear: What if parenthood is not what everyone says it should be? Many haunted home narratives interrogate the myth of blissful parenthood that is synonymous with so much of the suburban promise by featuring troubled children. While some are clearly evil, others are more of a conduit, either the first to sense the malignant presence or a vehicle possessed by the malignant presence. In all cases, the fault is on the parents for having failed to protect their child.

One of the ripple effects of traditional gender expectations enforced during the 1950s—and still prevalent today—is the idea that all women are meant to be (good) mothers. If a woman is not a good mother, if a woman is not happy as a mother, if a woman has difficulties with a child, societal stereotyping indicates that there is something wrong with her. In the book *Mastering Fear: Women,*

Emotions, and Contemporary Horror, Rikke Schubart explores the idea that the maternal instinct might actually be a myth constructed by society and enforced on women. Schubart specifically examines the way this myth is presented and interrogated in horror movies, many of which depict "the struggle to live up to the ideals of essential motherhood" (180). If a child turns out badly (demonic, a serial killer, or just plain problematic), that is often seen as the fault of the mother, who is negligent, selfish, and/or deficient.

Schubert provides *The Babadook* (Jennifer Kent, 2014) as an example. In the film, Amelia (Essie Davis) loves her son, Samuel (Noah Wiseman), even if she also sometimes hates him, but is increasingly unable to care for him. In an interview with Hugh Ryan for *Vice*, the director, Jennifer Kent, explains that she wanted to make a film about how "motherhood is hard" and women can "lose themselves," exploring "the big lie that we're told—that motherhood is just great and fulfilling and rewarding." Not only does Amelia reject many of the traditional aspects of mothering, such as nurturing, selflessness, and patience, but she even rejects her son directly, ignoring him and avoiding his hugs.

In *We Need to Talk About Kevin* (Lynne Ramsay, 2011), Tilda Swinton portrays Eva, an accomplished travel writer who marries and moves from the city to a house in the suburbs at her new husband's urging. When Franklin (John C. Reilly) moves his wife and child into their new suburban house—a move that foreshadows doom, oppression, and misery for Eva—he declares, "Here we are, guys! Our very own castle!" In his mind, he has accomplished the American dream: wife, child, house. However, in this new stage of life, Eva, formerly an adventuress, never travels and rarely leaves the house. She is trapped within her castle, having exchanged her freedom for the bonds of suburban motherhood.

The suburbs do not offer Eva the bliss and peacefulness they usually promise, and even the pleasures that are supposed to accompany motherhood are also noticeably absent. Kevin (Ezra Miller), her first child, veers between difficult and sociopathic, playing nice whenever the father is around but tormenting Eva when they are alone. She tries all the traditional mothering techniques but each time is rebuffed with condescension and/or malice. There might not be a supernatural component to this movie, but Kevin is pure evil. Eva's husband refuses to acknowledge what is happening, his disbelief reinforcing her isolation. Kevin eventually exposes his true colors to everyone by killing his father, his sister, and a group of several fellow high-school students. In what might be the cruelest twist of the film, the other residents of the town blame Eva for her son's behavior. After all, she should have been a better mother!

In *The Disappointments Room*, the implicit message is that Dana Barrow (Kate Beckinsale) deserves to be punished not only for the accidental death of her baby (failure #1) but also for the near killing of her son (failure #2), as well as for failing to release or protect the spirit of young Laura (failure #3), who died in the house during the 1800s. Her maternal instincts fail three times over. The family's initial move from Brooklyn, New York, to a dilapidated mansion in the North Carolina countryside is presented as a fresh start, an attempt to distract them-selves from the recent traumatic death of their infant daughter. Dana's husband, David (Mel Raido), refers to himself and Dana as the "lord and lady of the manor," utterly thrilled by their new life. Dana, in contrast, begins to see disturbing things shortly after their arrival in the new house, which has been abandoned since the death of Judge Ernest Blacker (Gerald McRaney) in the nineteenth century.

One of the first incidents starts with Dana observing a light turning on in an unexplained room in the attic that is not mentioned in the blueprints. When she goes to inves-tigate, the door slams shut behind her, locking her in for what, to her, feels like hours. By the time she manages to escape, face tear stained, makeup smudged, on the verge of hysterics, she stumbles down the stairs and into the living room, where a black-and-white movie plays on the television. Over the sound of Dana's rapid breathing, we hear a man say from the television, "That, gentlemen, is my wife—mad and the offspring of a mad family," as if introducing Dana herself.

Dana stares in shock at her husband and son, Lucas (Duncan Joiner), who play together as if everything were normal. "Where were you?" she asks her husband, her voice catching, everything about her on the verge of collapse. "I needed you, David." He looks back at her, confused. "I'm right here. I've been right here." For him, it is as if no time at all has passed. He has no idea what she is talking about when she explains that she was locked up "for hours and hours." Lucas also insists that they did not hear anything.

Temporarily speechless, Dana tries to make sense of the obvious discrepancy between her version of events and theirs. David walks over to her and asks if she has been having trouble sleeping. She shakes her head, insisting that she is *not* having trouble sleeping, angry that this is how he would dismiss her, and begging him not to look at her like that. "Like what?" David asks, but Lucas interjects: "Don't get sick again, Mommy," he implores her, not only introducing the possibility that she might be sick now, that this might all be in her head, but also pointing out that this has *already happened*, that she had been sick before and so could easily get sick again.

Dana insists that she is not sick, that she has never felt better—despite the fact that she looks terrified and distraught. But then the kitchen timer goes off, and she flinches as if slapped. It is obvious that she is not doing well. Her brain struggles to make sense of the fact that she put the food in the oven, that she set the timer, and that the timer had only just gone off, indicating that she was not actually gone for long, despite the hours and hours she seemingly spent locked in the attic. Not only does her husband doubt her, but now she doubts herself, as well.

The next day, Dana is in the throes of a nightmare. She jolts awake and heads to the bathroom to extract some prescription pills from the medicine cabinet. However, upon further reflection, she dumps all the pills in the bottle down the toilet and goes back to sleep. The implication, of course, is that she needs that medication, and so by flushing it down the toilet, she makes her mental state all the more unstable.

Interestingly, despite all the supposed instability, Dana is the main breadwinner in the family. However, despite the fact that she has the more high-profile job, she is still the one who unpacks and sets up the kitchen, who is primarily in charge of child care, who does the cooking, and who is constantly disbelieved. Halfway through the film, an argument between Dana and David demonstrates this power conflict. When contractor Ben Phillips (Lucas Till) shows up on the family's property, offering his services to help repair a massive leak, Dana is skeptical, reluctant to hand over the job. However, David walks in, straightaway asking Ben when he can start. Dana interjects, explaining that that "is still up in the air." David gestures to the mess accumulating as a result of the leak, telling his wife that they should probably act quickly. Despite the fact that, as an architect, she is in charge of all renovations, David tells Ben that they would like him to start as soon as possible.

Later that evening, Dana tells her husband that she wants to leave the house, that "something is not right." He replies by telling her that she just needs to "adjust." He emphasizes that it is "not the house" and blames inadequate medication. She insists he is wrong, but he will not budge, demanding that they stay at least a year, justifying it as falling under Lucas's need for stability. "In a year's time," he continues, "you're going to look back at this and know that this move was the right thing to do" (as a mother). As David heads off for a work trip, he tells five-year-old Lucas to look after his mother. Clearly, Dana is such a mess that she needs her own child, who is not even in first grade, to keep an eye on her.

Once David leaves, Dana goes to the local historical society to find more information on her house and, specifically, about the secret attic room. Hearing the words as she says them, Dana dismisses her own thoughts as "ridiculous." However, Ms. Judith (Marcia De Rousse), who runs the historical society, tells Dana that it sounds like she has a "disappointments room." A disappointments room, Judith explains, is where wealthy families would conceal disabled children so as not to be embarrassed by them. Sometimes, even the "very existence" of that child would be kept a secret. Locked in that room, tended to only "by the parents or perhaps a trusted service," the child would remain concealed from the world until death would come at last. "Some say their spirits could remain behind," Judith continues, "so I've been researching the presence of disturbed spirits in these old homes . . ." She trails off. "And . . . I think I've watched *Poltergeist* too many times," she concludes, laughing it off. "People say I'm full of shit and whiskey." She seems ready to dismiss her own observations just as easily as everyone else already has.

A few scenes later, in a flashback, Dana lies on the floor of the bathroom, tugging a razor blade along the inside of her left arm. We then cut to David in his therapist's office, explaining that he fears that Dana "is slipping." Clearly, the juxtaposition from one scene to the next emphasizes Dana's precarious mental state. David goes on to tell his therapist that Dana "thinks odd things are going on in the house," that she has "started to imagine things that aren't really happening again." With this statement, he not only emphasizes that Dana has a pattern of mental illness but also demonstrates his inability to see what she sees or, beyond that, to believe her. Interestingly, the therapist attributes Dana's difficulties to "being up in that big house, way outside of the city." The actual problem, he argues, is the isolation of their new house, and the solution is to have friends over. Rather than acknowledge the possibility that what Dana sees is actually happening, David dismisses it as mental illness, while the therapist dismisses it as loneliness.

The following night, Dana notices that the attic light has once again gone on. When she peers in the room, she sees Judge Blacker hovering over his wife (Mrs. Blacker, played by Jennifer Leigh Mann), who is feeding their daughter. "I will put her out of her misery," whispers Judge Blacker to his wife, holding a hammer over the head of their daughter. "We have allowed this curse to linger too long." His wife implores him not to, but he swings the hammer into his daughter's head, over and over, cracking her skull and sending her to the floor.

Horrified, Dana watches in stunned silence as the Judge decrees, "She will embarrass me no more," tossing the hammer on the floor to land beside his huddled wife. At this point, the Judge notices Dana and walks over to whisper in her ear. "You are a miserable mother," he says—note that this comes from a man who has just killed his daughter with a hammer—"and you will fail again: a daughter and now a dead son." The Judge orders his dog to attack Dana before walking away to find Lucas. Dana wrestles with the dog as the Judge holds a pillow over Lucas's head to suffocate him. Grabbing the hammer on the floor, she runs to Lucas's bedroom and hits the Judge in the head over and over with the hammer.

However, when David, hearing the screams, runs into the room, there is no sign of the Judge. Lucas is alone in bed, and his mother is attacking a pillow with the hammer. David grabs his son, pulling him to safety, as Dana runs off, distraught. David shouts at her, asking "what the fuck" was she thinking, is she out of her mind, and is she "trying to destroy everything" they had together? Dana reveals to her husband that she can no longer tell what is and is not real. Moments later, she also reveals that she killed her baby by rolling over on top of her while sleeping. Her husband tries to comfort her, but the fact remains that Dana killed one child and almost killed another. As if killing one's children were not bad enough, we cut to an aerial shot of the room, which is in a state of total disarray—another mark against Dana as a wife and mother.

As David and Dana head back to the city, Dana looks over and sees Judge Ernest Blacker standing at the window, watching them leave. Despite the fact that David had removed the door, the very last shot of the movie is of the door slamming shut on the disappointments room. The implication is clear: Dana has failed to take care of both her children, as well as failing to rectify the trauma committed earlier in the Blacker mansion, leaving the ghost of Laura locked in for all eternity. There is no final victory. If only she had been a better mother . . .

Another example of a "bad mother" occurs in *Case 39* (Christian Alvart, 2009). Renée Zellweger plays Emily Jenkins, a social worker who adopts Lilith Sullivan (Jodelle Ferland), a young girl she believes to have been abused. Initially reluctant to do so, Emily explains that it would not be a good idea because she works all day, is "hardly ever home," and, most importantly, is "just not mom material." Emily still ends up adopting Lilith. When the girl proves to be highly troubled, Emily goes back to the caseworker (Cynthia Stevenson) to ask for help. The caseworker merely says, "She's your responsibility. Make it work." Emily protests that she has no idea how to make it work, but the caseworker is unsympathetic, telling Emily she just needs the right coping skills, as if an able mother would be able to deal effortlessly with a demonic child. When Emily tells Detective Barron (Ian McShane) that there is something wrong with Lilith, he dismisses her, arguing that even if Lilith is damaged, deceitful, and manipulative, that still does not make her a demon. He accuses Emily of trying to run away from the responsibility of raising a child. Even Lilith, during a climactic conflict near the end of the film, when it is clear that Emily is right about Lilith and her demonic powers, lectures Emily, telling her that they "need to learn healthier ways of resolving conflict," again implying that if Emily had the right coping skills, there would be no problem.

Katherine Guerra points out that many contemporary horror films feature an "elusive, reluctant, and 'resistant' mother," writing that "the antithesis of maternal love isn't possessiveness, hate, or violence, but instead ambivalence." In other words, terror comes from the mother who does not do or care enough. Guerra provides the film *Hereditary* (Ari Aster, 2018) as an example. *Hereditary* not only depicts the troubled relationship that mother Annie (Toni Collette) has with her children but also looks at the various ways in which she tries to abandon the role of motherhood. In one particularly upsetting moment, Annie shouts at her son Peter (Alex Wolff), "I never wanted to be your mother."

Hereditary examines the repercussions of the death of Annie's mother, not only commenting on the adverse affects of isolation on Annie's psyche, as well as the adverse effects of "playing house" in the suburbs, but also emphasizing the repercussions of unresolved grief and trauma. Annie does not know how to deal with the trauma of her mother's death, a shock that is further exacerbated by her daughter's death. Annie and her husband, Steven (Gabriel Byrne), do not know how to communicate with each other properly; they literally cannot hear what the other person is saying. When Peter kills his sister, he is left to pick up the pieces on his own, with no suggestion of therapy or any other kind of professional assistance.

In what appears to be a clear reference to the real-life artist Laurie Simmons, Annie is an artist specializing in miniatures. Simmons has spent decades crafting miniature dioramas of women in the home, as well as shooting portraits of dolls made to look like real girls, in order to comment on how women and girls are portrayed and encouraged to behave. Annie similarly builds little houses and hospice centers and nursery schools, all resembling the real-life buildings surrounding her suburban home. She even briefly works as a photographer for a dollhouse miniature company. Ari Aster, the film's director, frequently blends the dollhouses with the real houses, making it unclear at times whether the audience sees a life-size home or a miniature one. This blurring of real and artificial is also emphasized in the way some of the characters are posed. For instance, at the end of the movie, it is unclear if the cultists are actual human beings or dolls, since they are posed stiffly and there are mannequins nearby.

One of the messages behind this blurring of real and artificial is that, while Annie is excellent at crafting domesticity on the small scale (where it does not matter), her efforts on the larger scale leave much to be desired. In one of the first lines of dialogue, Annie's daughter, Charlie (Milly Shapiro), asks who will take care of her now that the grandmother is dead. Annie, shocked, insists that she will take care of her daughter, but Charlie does not appear to be convinced. It turns out that Charlie is right not to feel safe. A short time later, Annie sends Charlie to a high-school party with her older brother, Peter, which is totally inappropriate and which results in Charlie's death.

The movie continues to emphasize what a poor mother Annie is: her husband often prepares dinner; Annie only had a child because her mother was pressuring her to keep it; Steven frequently needs to protect Peter from his mother. Annie even recounts a traumatic night in which she woke up to find herself standing over her son, carrying paint thinner and matches, prepared to set him ablaze. Annie is also a poor wife, as evident through many of these same examples and also because of the fact that her husband is forced to sleep on the couch. Her actions lead directly to his death—ironically by fire, much as she almost killed her son.

Unsurprisingly, Steven refuses to believe that his wife's fears might be valid as she begins to figure out that something terrible is happening within her home and that supernatural forces are at play. He dismisses her protestations, telling her that she is sick, using his career as a psychiatrist to lend legitimacy to his claims. The fact that Annie is so isolated compounds the problem. There are no nearby neighbors, and she works from home, emphasizing just how isolating and oppressive the life of a suburban mother can be.

In *Home* (Frank Lin, 2016) one of the key turning points occurs when young Tia asks her older half sister, Carrie (Kerry Knuppe), "Why do you hate me?" and says Carrie does not want her there. Since Carrie, in the absence of Tia's parents, is the makeshift mother/caretaker, this exchange echoes countless films like *Hereditary*, *We Need to Talk About Kevin*, and *The Disappointments Room*, in which the mother fails in her job as mother. Carrie's inability to refute Tia's claim—her initial response is awkward silence, followed by the double negative of "I don't not want you here" and the statement "I don't . . . dislike you"—further emphasizes that Carrie is a bad "mother." Carrie does not have proper maternal instincts, but neither does Tia's actual mother. The main reason Carrie is in charge is because Tia's real parents have left! And Tia's mother is a lesbian! Who marries an atheist! The fact that everyone forgets to pick up Tia from school on the day she is seemingly possessed is of little surprise. With such neglectful mother figures, is it any surprise that Tia would be possessed by a demon? With such neglectful mother figures, Tia does not stand a chance.

In the Netflix adaptation of *The Haunting of Hill House*, Olivia is unable to make her children feel safe. In the episode "Screaming Meemies" (Netflix, 2018) young Nell (Violet McGraw) worries about having bad dreams in which Olivia kills her and young Luke (Julian Hilliard). "What if I dream that you send us away into the dark, and we get hurt?" Nell continues, adding more detail for her confused mother. "You send us away, out into the dark, and my heart breaks right in half, and I can't feel anything happy for weeks and months and years, until I can't stand it anymore, and I have to die." Luke interjects, "And what if I'm so sad and scared of the dark out there that I put poison in me? I poison myself for years and years until my blood turns into poison and my body breaks down." The two of them, with their childlike innocence, are predicting what will happen to their future selves, with the emphasis being that it is Olivia who is at fault. Nell adds, "You send us out there into the dark, and the dark gets us, a piece at a time, over years and years and years. . . . And it was you that killed us because you sent us out there." A mother has one job: to keep her kids safe. And Olivia fails. "Would you wake us up from a dream like that," Nell asks, "and keep us safe?" Olivia, shocked by these questions, responds with "of course," but Nell continues: "But *are* we safe with you, Mommy? Are we really?" Because of the nonlinear narrative of the series, we already know the answer to that question, and no, they are not. Like Tia, they do not stand a chance.

In the next scene, Mrs. Dudley (Annabeth Gish) stumbles on Olivia in a random nook. Olivia explains that she is hiding. What is unspoken is that Olivia is hiding from her own children, something only a bad mother would do. Mrs. Dudley reveals to Olivia that her son Steven (Paxton Singleton) is worried about her, something that a young child should never have to feel. Olivia, rather than addressing the fact that her son is worried about her, tells Mrs. Dudley that she is terrified at the prospect of her children leaving the home, venturing into the world beyond the walls of the house. The irony, of course, is that the children are in far more danger from the world *within* the walls of their home. Mrs. Dudley tells Olivia to stand firm, to protect her children, to get them out of the house, but of course, Olivia fails at this. She is too weak to protect her children.

Similarly, in *The Other Side of the Door* (Johannes Roberts, 2016), Maria (Sarah Wayne Callies) is unable to perform her duties as a mother. In fact, the premise of the entire film is what happens when a mother fails to protect her children. The initial incident that triggers the primary conflict of the film is Maria's choice to save her daughter, Lucy (Sofia Rosinsky), and not her son, Oliver (Logan Creran), following a car accident, leaving her son to drown. Consumed by guilt and isolated in their new home in India, Maria at first tries to kill herself, thereby abandoning her second child. When this attempt fails, Maria's housekeeper, Piki (Suchitra Pillai), offers Maria the opportunity to speak to Oliver one final time. Piki tells Maria about an abandoned temple where the dead and the living can speak with each other through a door. The caveat: Maria must not open the door.

Of course, Maria, as a bad mother, opens the door, thus preventing Oliver from being properly reincarnated and bringing out his restless soul to wander through the world of the living, where he eventually possesses Lucy. Maria has now done irreparable damage to *both* her children. Her husband, Michael (Jeremy Sisto), believes none of what Maria tells him, convinced that this is more mental instability. He even locks her in a room for her own good, telling her that everything will be okay, but moments later, his own daughter stabs him and the family dog. As Michael bleeds out on the kitchen floor, Lucy scolds him, telling him that he is making a mess and that "Mommy will be mad," as if to draw attention to how screwed up Maria's priorities are. Maria's only way to rectify things is to offer up her own life, but, unfortunately, this merely opens up the cycle for Michael to make the same mistake at the temple as she did, thus destroying the life of yet more family members.

In the made-for-television movie *Amityville 4: The Evil Escapes* (Sandor Stern, 1989), which aired on NBC, Nancy Evans (Patty Duke) and her three children, Amanda (Zoe Trilling), Brian (Aron Eisenberg), and Jessica (Brandy Gold), are forced to move in with Nancy's mother, Alice (Jane Wyatt). While the obvious reason for this is the death of Nancy's husband, it is clear that Nancy's poor mothering abilities are also to blame. After all, the family's lack of financial security lies with her. Nancy even tells her own mother, "It's my fault for not being better prepared to earn a living." The father did the right thing and made sure to leave life insurance, but because of Nancy's lack of financial prowess, the family is forced to move in with Alice. In addition, Jessica, the youngest child, is having a hard time dealing with the death of her father, and Nancy is frequently told by others that she is making things worse for her daughter. When Amanda implores her mother to move them elsewhere, Nancy refuses, saying that they "don't have that luxury" and that she is "doing the best" she can, which is clearly not good enough.

A twist on the "bad mother" trope occurs in *Malicious* (Michael Winnick, 2018) when expectant parents James Harper (Luke Edwards) and Lisa (Bojana Novakovic) lose their baby before she is even born. The couple relocates to a rural town following James's appointment at the local college. As he leaves for his first day at his new school, he begs Lisa to be careful, and she replies, "I am pregnant, not breakable." Unfortunately, she fails to take into account how fragile her baby is. Soon after James leaves for work on his first day, Lisa hears the sounds of a baby crying. Confused, she quickly heads upstairs and looks in the crib. A young girl with heavy makeup is inside. The next shot shows us Lisa lying on the floor of the nursery, blood seeping out from between her legs. We then see Lisa and James in the hospital, Lisa hooked up to a hospital bed, as a nurse or doctor explains that Lisa suffered a miscarriage and that she will not be able to have children any more. Such a bad mother . . .

When Lisa and James return home from the hospital, Lisa's visions intensify, and she continues to see the same

girl who had been in the crib right before Lisa's miscarriage. Lisa begs James to bring fellow professor Dr. Clark
(Delroy Lindo) to the house, insisting that he can help
them since he is one of the top paranormal researchers in
the country. James, unsurprisingly, is skeptical, ready to
dismiss his wife as crazy and emotional, but he still com-
plies with her request.

Clark places recording devices throughout the home in
an attempt to determine which evil forces are at play and
what those forces want. There is no question for him that
the forces are there. The first audio recording is of a girl's
voice saying, "Mom, mother, mommy, mama, madre"
over and over. When Clark asks the voice who it is, the
voice answers, "Lisa Junior," which is what James and Lisa
had taken to calling their future child before losing her to
the miscarriage. Upon this revelation, all the lightbulbs
break, plunging the house into darkness. We hear a child
running and laughing upstairs. Clark asks Lisa Junior
what it will take to put her back into the box from which
she supposedly came. Lisa, ever the defiant child/spirit,
whispers, "You don't." At this point, the recording devices
hum with electricity, the monitor growing brighter and
brighter until Clark twitches, as if electrocuted. When
he comes to, he slowly removes his dark glasses, and his
eyes—formerly blue, foggy, unseeing—appear brown
and sharp and functional. Despite being blind in our

conventional reality, Clark can see in other dimensions. This ability allows him to see the entity that killed Lisa and James's unborn daughter, possessed her spirit, and then took her place. James asks how they can get rid of the entity, but Clark just shakes his head. He explains that nowhere is safe anymore because the evil spirit will follow Lisa wherever she goes.

The poster for the film features the same child whom Lisa found in the crib, her face masked in shadow, nightgown seemingly blood stained, beneath the tag line, "Children are a gift from heaven," except that "heaven" has been crossed out, the word "Hell" written in its stead. When asked about the film in an interview with Borys Kit for the *Hollywood Reporter*, executive producer Shaun Redick explained that "the fear and the fragility of having a newborn weighs on every couple," but in *Malicious*, "those terrors are heightened in unexpected ways." It is not merely that the terrors are heightened in this film, however. It is that the terror has expanded to the fear not just of losing a child but also of creating a child who is actually evil. And you can never escape your own child.

Similarly, for an innocent child, it can be hard to escape your family when thoroughly isolated. In Robert Eggers's movie *The Witch* (2015), both parents, in their frenzy to accuse their eldest daughter of witchcraft, destroy their family. The film tells the story of William (Ralph Ineson);

his wife, Katherine (Kate Dickie); and their children, recent settlers to New England in the early seventeenth century. The family, exiled from their Puritan colony for reasons that are not explained, creates a new home for themselves in an isolated area alongside an ominous forest. Before too long, however, the youngest child disappears, the crops fail, and any hope for a fresh start collapses. To make things worse, the family—totally removed from any other human contact—blames Thomasin (Anya Taylor-Joy), the oldest daughter, for the baby's disappearance, calling her a witch and deeming her responsible for all of the family's problems. The most disturbing element of the movie is the way the family turns on Thomasin, quick to blame her without any proof.

Jess Joho, in her review of the film, writes that it explores "the horrific trauma inherent to being a woman in 17th century America." However, while the film does not paint a rosy picture of the life afforded to Katherine or to any of the other family members, it is Thomasin who bears the brunt of the suffering. It is Thomasin who is accused of being a witch. It is not just her femininity or her sexuality that make her an easy target. It, specifically, is her youth. Her childlike status, combined with the twinges of blossoming adulthood, makes her an easy target. While some viewers may see the film's ending, in which Thomasin joins the coven of witches living in the woods, as empowering, it is significant to remember that Thomasin has no say in that decision. As a child, living in a cursed place, she is given no other options. After all, her mother tried to kill her, blaming Thomasin for all of the tragedy that has plagued the family. When Thomasin joins the coven, it is because she has nowhere else to go. How else could she not just escape her family but survive?

BAD PARENTS AND VULNERABLE KIDS

One of the most famous possessed children in Hollywood cinema history is Regan (Linda Blair) in *The Exorcist* (William Friedkin, 1973). In the film, the actress Chris MacNeil (Ellen Burstyn) temporarily relocates to Washington, DC, with her daughter while on a shoot and rents a home for them. Since the events that occur are clearly tied to that rental property, this brings blame back to MacNeil, who, by prioritizing her career, brought the two of them to that home in the first place and failed to protect her daughter within it. Before there is even a hint of demonic possession, a candle goes wild in the attic, and we hear scratching sounds that are never explained. These strange occurrences serve to foreshadow the strangeness occurring within Regan. After playing with a Ouija board, Regan begins acting out, shouting obscene words, peeing on the living-room floor, and displaying superhuman strength. At the same time, strange activity in the house intensifies as objects move suddenly, seemingly by themselves. It becomes clear to all observers that something is terribly wrong with Regan. The demon within her becomes increasingly violent, and the death toll mounts until Father Karras (Jason Miller) sacrifices himself in order to cure Regan.

The film *Annabelle: Creation* (David F. Sandberg, 2017), a prequel to the 2014 *Annabelle* (John R. Leonetti), features possessed and tormented children in spades. Samuel and Esther Mullins (Anthony LaPaglia and Miranda Otto), grieving for the loss of their seven-year-old daughter, Annabelle, turn their home into an orphanage for six girls. It is later revealed that the main reason for their generosity is their guilt over the fact that they accidentally attracted a demon to their family when they begged for some entity to restore Annabelle, however briefly. Janice (Talitha Bateman), one of the orphans, unknowingly releases the demon while exploring the home. The demon begins to torment the girls, possessing Janice and turning her into a killer. To make things worse, Janice manages to escape, ending up in another orphanage, from which she is subsequently adopted. Years later, she ends up murdering those parents, as well—all because Samuel and Esther foolishly summoned a demon for their own selfish reasons.

Another parent who jeopardizes his family by prioritizing his career is Ellison Oswalt (Ethan Hawke) in *Sinister* (Scott Derrickson, 2012). Oswalt moves his family without their knowledge into a home where the previous family had been brutally murdered. His ulterior motive is to write a true-crime best seller about the events that had transpired there, a choice that will prove deadly. Unfortunately, the home Oswalt has chosen is not just the site of a horrific crime but also the location of an evil Babylonian deity named Bughuul. This deity kills entire families except for one child, whose soul he claims. By moving the family into this particular home, Oswalt has put them all in Bughuul's direct line of fire. Once Oswalt realizes his mistake, he quickly moves the family to another home, but it is too late. This provides an amusing twist to the age-old "why don't they move?" question in virtually every haunted home narrative. In this case, the family *does* move, but that is precisely what seals their fate. In this particular narrative, the evil spirit specifically destroys the family after they have moved. Bughuul has already set his sights on the Oswalt family and, specifically, the daughter, Ashley (Clare Foley). Controlled by the evil deity, Ashley kills the rest of her family before joining the rest of the missing children.

The film's sequel, *Sinister 2* (Ciaran Foy, 2015), also revolves around Bughuul and his tribe of evil children.

While the primary threat initially seems to be the abusive father/husband from which the family is hiding, the home itself provides an even greater threat. The film stresses that the mother is at least partly to blame for not protecting the children from the father's violence, while, at the same time, the mother clearly does not protect the children from Bughuul and his minions, seemingly oblivious to their presence as she moves the family into this haunted home. When she is warned that the adjoining church, which she uses as her studio, had been the site of a ritual murder, she does not care. The mother's failures to parent properly are numerous.

Young Dylan (Robert Daniel Sloan), the quieter and more submissive of the two boys, begins seeing Bughuul's children. One of the creepiest (Milo, played by Lucas Jade Zumann) regularly forces Dylan to spend his nights watching the same Super 8 films Oswalt discovered. Dylan, as the more sensitive child, also briefly sees Bughuul, adding to the nightmares he is already having as a result of his father's abuse. Dylan's life is made even more unpleasant by the increasing aggression of his brother, Zach (Dartanian Sloan), who is jealous over all the extra attention Dylan is receiving. It turns out that Zach is the actual target of Bughuul's group. It is Zach who is "turned," and it is Zach who tries to kill his family. Unfortunately for Zach, he fails, thwarted by the Deputy

(James Ransone), and is then destroyed by Bughuul in retribution.

Yet another seemingly ordinary family moves to a new home in the suburbs in *Insidious* (James Wan, 2010). Shortly after arriving in the house, Dalton (Ty Simpkins) makes his way to the attic unsupervised (bad parents), where he falls into a coma. Once he is brought back home from the hospital, still in a coma, inexplicable and frightening events begin to occur. As usual, these are frightening events that mother Renai (Rose Byrne) can see and that father Josh (Patrick Wilson) ignores—even though, as we discover later, Dalton inherited his supernatural abilities from his father. Eventually, Renai is attacked in the house, and only then does Josh agree to move. Unfortunately, Renai continues to see supernatural activity at the new location because the evil has already latched onto the family. Josh's mother, Lorraine (Barbara Hershey), who can also see the supernatural activity, realizes that the family needs a demonologist to help with the situation and summons the psychic Elise Reiner (Lin Shaye). When Elise arrives at the home, she, too, can see the demon figure visible to Renai and Lorraine.

Elise explains that it is not the house that is haunted but, rather, the boy. He is not in a coma in the traditional sense of the term. Rather, he is trapped in a realm full of tortured souls. Since he has temporarily left his physical body, evil spirits can then use it, which is the explanation for all the frightening occurrences that have plagued the family. In order to save Dalton, Josh—who has the same supernatural ability to travel to other mental planes as his son—must go into the same realm to find Dalton and bring him back. In contrast, the mother is so useless that she cannot even rescue her child. Although Josh brings Dalton back, the film ends with Josh possessed by a demon, killing Elise and terrifying Renai. The savior has become the threat, reminding us once again of the vulnerability that women and children experience in the home.

Don't Be Afraid of the Dark (Troy Dixey, 2010) combines various aspects of troubled and vulnerable children in its haunted home narrative. Sally (Bailee Madison), the daughter of estranged parents (aka bad parents), is sent to live with her father, Alex (Guy Pearce), and his new partner, Kim (Katie Holmes), in their huge new house. Sally, naturally, is the first to sense the evil forces at play, and they target her precisely because of her susceptibility and trusting nature. After all, as a little girl, she is an easy mark. It is precisely because Sally is a difficult child, angry at her parents for the collapse of their marriage, that she refuses to follow the rules suggested by Alex and Kim and engages directly with the evil forces. While she thinks they just want to be friends, once the evil spirits have leveraged her to gain access to the house, their true intentions are revealed.

The house's caretaker, an elderly man played by Jack Thompson, is also susceptible to the evil forces, partly because of his years with the house but also because his age—on the opposite end of the spectrum—makes him more vulnerable. He knows that the house is not safe for Sally and recognizes that she has been targeted, but Alex and Kim refuse, at first, to comply (bad parents). About an hour into the movie, Kim finally figures out that something dangerous is afoot and pleads with Alex to leave. Alex predictably refuses to go, saying that every cent he has is tied up in the house, prioritizing finances over his family's safety. Eventually, Kim—who is not even Sally's biological parent—pays for Alex's stubborn refusal with her life, sacrificing herself in order for Sally to survive.

Neglectful guardians are to blame in *The Innocents* (Jack Clayton, 1961), based on Henry James's novella *The Turn of the Screw* (1898). Miss Giddens (Deborah Kerr) is a governess recently hired to supervise two children, Miles (Martin Stephens) and Flora (Pamela Frankin). As the movie progresses, Miss Giddens starts to suspect that ghosts possess the children, as well as the house. Unfortunately, as yet another neglectful guardian, the children's uncle has no interest in them, so Miss Giddens and the children are isolated at their country estate, along with

Mrs. Grose (Megs Jenkins), the housekeeper. Miss Giddens begins to see a man and a woman whom she manages to identify as Miss Jessel (Clytie Jessop) and Peter Quint (Peter Wyngarde), the former governess and the uncle's former valet, both of whom are now deceased. Mrs. Grose explains to Miss Giddens that Miss Jessel and Quint had had an inappropriate affair, acting in a sexually explicit manner in front of the other members of the household—another parenting failure. Miss Giddens, observing the oddly flirtatious dynamic between Miles and Flora, begins to suspect that Miss Jessel and Quint have taken over the bodies of Miles and Flora so as to continue their affair after death. Once again, the vulnerable children are pawns.

In *Amityville 6: It's About Time* (Tony Randel, 1992), Jacob Sterling (Stephen Macht), who builds suburban housing developments, lives with his two kids in one of those cookie-cutter developments. The basic premise of the film is that Jacob brings home a clock he found in one of the homes he demolished for a new development in Long Island, the infamous Amityville house. The clock, naturally, contains the evil spirit that had once haunted that tragic home. Jacob's wife has passed away, and he is a single parent, relying inappropriately on the assistance of his ex-girlfriend, Andrea (Shawn Weatherly), to help with child care as well as to participate in the occasional one-night stand (another bad parent). As a result, the children act out in various ways that intensify over the course of the film. For instance, in a classic sign of neglectful parenting, teenage daughter Lisa (Megan Ward) grows more sexual and manipulative as her clothes become more and more revealing. Rusty (Damon Martin), the son, is supposedly a troublemaker, frequently targeted by the police whenever anything goes wrong, but other than skipping school, he seems to be better behaved than his sister, who, as she grows increasingly possessed by evil forces, even kills her high-school paramour.

In haunted home narratives, it is often the vulnerable child who possesses a keener sense of intuition or malleability, allowing the demon to use them as a portal for communication. Little girls and sensitive boys are often seen as the easiest prey. For example, in *The Haunting of Hill House*, the characters most vulnerable to the effects of the haunting are the two youngest children, Nell and Luke. Rusty, despite the punk-rock posters and the dangling earring, is actually a sensitive kid. He is the one who has a relationship with an elderly woman who quickly identifies the evil spirit at work. He is also the first one in his family to identify what is actually going on in their house, even though no one believes him. Andrea, in fact, tells Rusty that the "only evil force" in the house is him. Rusty tries to convince her, explaining that the evil force is now "in everything," as it tries "to make this house its home." Rusty insists that the reason his father is suffering from the aftereffects of a dog bite has nothing to do with needing to go to a doctor. Rather, "he's suffering up there because of what's in this house," and the rest of the family needs "to get out." Nothing he says convinces Andrea, who insists that she cannot believe him.

Sometimes, as in *The Darkness* (Greg McLean, 2016) and *Rose Red* (ABC, 2002), this keen sense is explicitly tied to autism. In *The Darkness*, mother Bronny (Radha Mitchell), when trying to understand why her autistic son is so vulnerable to evil spirits, even reads articles titled "Autistic Children: Magnets for Ghosts and Spirits," "How Children with Autism Tap into Psychic Abilities," and "Investigations: Autism and Children Subjected to Paranormal." The more vulnerable and sensitive the child, the more receptive the child is to evil spirits.

Carol Anne (Heather O'Rourke) is a similarly easy target in Tobe Hooper's classic film *Poltergeist* (1982). When the Freeling family moves into a planned suburban community where Steve Freeling (Craig T. Nelson) is a real estate developer, the family is initially excited about their brand-new home. Carol Anne, unable to sleep one night, begins talking to the television set. She does this again the following night, calling out without explanation, "They're here." Strange events begin to occur. Objects within the home move, break, and even attack family members, and then, without warning, Carol Anne is sucked into a demonic portal and is nowhere to be found. The only lingering sign is her voice coming from the television set. The rest of the movie revolves around the family's various attempts to retrieve Carol Anne from this cursed alternate dimension and their discovery that their home has been built above a cemetery. Of course, not only did the parents move the family there, but Steve was one of the real estate developers responsible for the community's existence! Whether explicitly stated or not, Carol Anne's predicament is her parents' fault.

The concept of little girls being sucked into portals within their suburban homes had already appeared twenty years earlier, in the Richard Matheson–penned episode of *The Twilight Zone* (CBS, 1959–64) titled "Little Girl Lost" (March 16, 1962). The Miller family—Chris (Robert Sampson), Ruth (Sarah Marshall), and their daughter, Tina (Tracey Stratford)—leads an utterly mundane life until Tina suddenly disappears. Much like in the later *Poltergeist*, the parents can hear their daughter but cannot find her. With the help of scientist Bill (Charles Aidman), they discover that Tina has somehow accessed another dimension from her bedroom. Whereas ghosts—and a disrespected cemetery—are to blame in *Poltergeist*, the culprit here is merely the interdimensional portal, providing the requisite proof that even the most banal suburban home can lead to hell and that even the most banal suburban home can prove dangerous for little girls, especially when parents are not properly attentive.

Even though horror films, much like melodramas, are often dismissed for their exaggerated plots and hyperbolic emotions, both types of film can often get to the heart of what is really happening in the home. While ghosts might not be a common feature in a new home, domesticity can come with many of the problems featured in haunted home narratives. Women are often dismissed as being overly emotional and unreliable. Men are frequently criticized for being distant, prioritizing professional life over personal. And as anyone who has a child knows, there are few things more exhausting than raising one. In contrast to the ideal of motherhood celebrated in mommy blogs and Instagram posts, suburbia and parenthood can be both stifling and demanding, oppressive and lonely, and even, for far too many women and children, violent and disappointing.

4

RACE, HORROR, AND THE HOME

In the suburban ideal of the cultural imagination, there are lush lawns and immaculate landscaping, children playing freely while women bake and smile. Husbands stream away for work in the morning and stream back home for dinner in the evening, flush with professional success. Cars drive slowly. They rarely honk. People smile and greet each other by name. Could this be perfection? However, the suburbs entice not only for what they offer but also for what (and whom) they exclude. Dolores Hayden, in her book *Redesigning the American Dream*, writes that US cities and housing were designed "to satisfy a nation of predominantly white, young, nuclear families, with father as breadwinner, mother as housewife, and children reared to emulate these same limited roles" (40). While the gender divisions are troubling, as discussed in chapter 3, also troubling is the emphasis on the category "white."

KEEPING THE SUBURBS WHITE

Through a variety of legal discriminatory techniques, the suburbs were preserved for white, young, nuclear families. For example, loan money was channeled away from minorities and toward white prospective home-owners. In 1935, the Home Owners' Loan Corporation (HOLC) defined certain neighborhoods as "minority neighborhoods"—because of the presence of African Americans or European immigrants, especially Jews— and made it an official policy to refuse to lend to residents of those neighborhoods, deeming it too risky. Those neighborhoods would literally be coded red on the maps the HOLC created, which is why this policy was called "redlining." It took until 1968 for the government to pass the Fair Housing Act, which finally banned this kind of racial discrimination. However, Black applicants are still turned away by banks at significantly higher rates than whites are.

The Federal Housing Administration (FHA) also refused to insure mortgages in or near Black neighborhoods and only subsidized builders who committed to selling their new homes exclusively to white people. The FHA further exacerbated the racism implicit in the HOLC's policies by establishing a rating system to evaluate which homes were a "worthwhile investment" and which residents were "credit worthy," writes Vincent J. Cannato in his article "A Home of One's Own." Unsurprisingly, white neighborhoods were often on the "credit worthy" side of the scale, while more ethnically diverse neighborhoods were deemed risky. In other words, the whiter the neighborhood (and the prospective homeowner), the easier to get a mortgage.

The FHA also endorsed covenants that prevented minorities from purchasing certain homes. These covenants were literal clauses in property deeds that stipulated that land (or homes) could not be sold to African Americans, *even if they could afford the down payment*. While these covenants had existed prior to the creation of the FHA, the support they received from the FHA allowed them to become even more widespread. Thus, the FHA and the HOLC successfully encouraged white Americans to relocate to the suburbs and become homeowners— while just as successfully discouraging minorities from doing the same.

The "justification" for these racist policies was that minority presence would decrease property values. However, as Richard Rothstein explains in his book *The Color of Law: A Forgotten History of How Our Government Segregated America*, the opposite was true. African Americans were often more willing to pay higher prices for available homes because so many homes were not available to them, and so they would cause property values to rise. Nonetheless, in an interview with Terry Gross on National Public Radio, Rothstein describes a particular development in Detroit where the FHA required the developer to build a "6-foot-high wall, cement wall, separating his development from a nearby African-American neighborhood to make sure that no African-Americans could even walk into that neighborhood" ("Forgotten"). In lieu of cement walls, the FHA also considered highways to be an acceptable way to separate minority neighborhoods from white neighborhoods.

While the number of African American suburbanites did increase between 1940 and 1960, the primary reason for this was "Negro expansion areas," developments established for the explicit purpose of housing African Americans. However, these developments were limited, and so housing was still difficult to find for African Americans and other nonwhites wishing to leave the city. By the early 1950s, only 2 percent of homes built with government-backed mortgages since World War II were occupied by African Americans or other minorities (Wiese 101). By 1960, the proportion of FHA mortgages given to African Americans and people of color was still 2 percent.

By the time the last home in Levittown, New York, was built in 1951, the development remained 100 percent white. In August 1957, William and Daisy Myers, a Black couple, and their children moved into Levittown, Pennsylvania, the only nonwhite residents in the community of seventeen thousand. As loosely re-created in *Suburbicon* (George Clooney, 2017), the family was tormented by years of violence and burning crosses before moving to Harrisburg, Pennsylvania. Unfortunately, in the years since, little has changed. Data from the US Census in 2017 indicates that Levittown, New York, is 75 percent white, 1 percent Black, and 15 percent Hispanic, while Levittown, Pennsylvania, is 88 percent white, 4 percent Black, and 6 percent Hispanic.

These statistics are not confined to Levittown developments. George Lipsitz traced the numbers of whites and Blacks leaving the cities and moving to the suburbs, observing that from 1960 to 1977, the number of whites living in the suburbs increased by twenty-two million. In contrast, the inner-city Black population grew by six million, while "the number of blacks living in suburbs increased by only 500,000 people. By 1993, 86 percent of suburban whites still lived in places with a black population below 1 percent" (343). In 2018, Aaron Glantz and Emmanuel Martinez wrote in the *Chicago Tribune* that the homeownership gap between whites and African Americans "is now wider than it was during the Jim Crow era." While not all affluent suburbs are primarily white, most certainly are.

KEEPING (HAUNTED) HOMES WHITE

While whiteness dominates in suburban neighborhoods offscreen, it also dominates in suburban neighborhoods on-screen. An overwhelming majority of haunted home narratives revolve around white protagonists—so overwhelming, in fact, that I only found two examples of Black homes being haunted, and one of those examples is a satire. Aviva Briefel and Sianne Ngai, in their article on the horror film *Candyman* (Bernard Rose, 1992) argue that "being frightened is paradoxically a sign of empowerment," as if the privilege of being haunted, much like the privilege of owning a home, is one reserved for white Americans (71).

The conspicuous lack of minority representation in haunted home narratives is explicitly dealt with by Eddie Murphy in his stand-up comedy special *Delirious* (Bruce Gowers, 1983). Although Murphy does not address why those whose houses are haunted are always white, he does raise the question of why those white residents stay. Murphy asks, "Why don't white people just leave the house when there's a ghost in the house? Ya'll stay in the house too fuckin' long. Just get the fuck out of the house. Very simple: there's a ghost in the house, get the fuck out." He specifically mentions the films *Poltergeist* (Tobe Hooper, 1982), in which the protagonists not only stay in the house but invite "more white people over" to help them deal with the situation, and *The Amityville Horror*, in which a ghost specifically warns the white family to get out, and yet they remain. Murphy retorts, "A ghost say get the fuck out, I would just trip the fuck out the door."

Fittingly, the title of Jordan Peele's directorial debut, *Get Out* (2017), was inspired by Eddie Murphy's routine. Peele talked to *Entertainment Tonight* about Murphy's comedy special, describing how Murphy compares the reaction of a white family to the reaction of a Black family to being in a haunted house and referring to it as "one of the best bits of all time." In the same interview, Peele also explains that one of his favorite parts of many horror films is the doubt that sinks in when protagonists wonder if they are imagining the strange things that are happening. Significantly and unsurprisingly, the doubting protagonist is most often the wife or mother.

However, in *Get Out*, the doubting protagonist is the African American photographer Chris Washington (Daniel Kaluuya). In another twist on the typical haunted home narrative, Chris's friend Rod (Lil Rel Howery) is disbelieved and mocked by the police, rather than the hysterical white woman filling that role. Whereas gender is usually used to justify not taking someone seriously, manipulating them for whatever end result, Peele uses race. And much as a woman's outsider status can enable her to perceive unusual situations more readily, Chris and Rod's Blackness enables them "to perceive that something sinister is going on," explains Peele (Chan).

Chris's white girlfriend, Rose Armitage (Allison Williams), reassures him that meeting her parents for the first time will be no big deal. After all, they would have voted for Obama's third term, if they could! The parents, Dean (Bradley Whitford), a neurosurgeon, and Missy (Catherine Keener), a psychiatrist specializing in hypnotherapy, seem superficially pleasant at first, except for their racially inappropriate comments. Even more disturbing, their housekeeper, Georgina (Betty Gabriel), and groundskeeper, Walter (Marcus Henderson), the only other African Americans at the home, appear to be somewhat lobotomized. Every attempt Chris makes to engage with them ends strangely. He quickly realizes that his concerns about Rose's parents not liking him severely underestimated the actual problems he would face with the family.

Soon, more white people (and one African American) arrive at the Armitage house for a party. Chris continues to have unsettling interaction after unsettling interaction. As he describes it to Rose, he says, "The people here, it's like they haven't met a Black person who doesn't work for them." One of the most bizarre interactions Chris has is with Andre Logan King (LaKeith Stanfield), who seems to have no connection to his African American heritage and is married to a much older white woman. Chris recognizes Andre, realizing that he has met him before but that Andre had an entirely different personality back then. This is because Andre, while having the same exterior, is now someone else inside. It turns out that the Armitage family is running a sinister operation out of their basement. The family takes the brains of white people and puts them in the bodies of carefully selected African Americans who are seen as a physical upgrade. They literally appropriate not only Black culture but also Black bodies. The man who wants Chris's body, for instance, is blind and wants Chris's eyes and artistic talent.

While the evil in *Get Out* is not connected to supernatural forces, since there are no demons at play, the core essence of the haunted home narrative—that the home is actually the most dangerous place in the world for the vulnerable—runs throughout the whole film. Also like the haunted home narrative, *Get Out* explores the evil that lies just behind beautiful, opulent, and supposedly safe surroundings, although what might be safe to white people is not always safe for Black people. Rod warns Chris, just a few minutes into the movie, "Don't go to a white girl's parents' house." Chris ignores his friend and hangs up the phone. Still, about halfway through the film, Chris tells Georgina, "All I know is, sometimes, if there's too many white people, I get nervous." Throughout the film, Chris becomes increasingly aware of just how threatening the Armitage home is for him. However, as nervous as he may get, he still does not try to leave until it is too late—the classic haunted house mistake. At the very end, Rod looks over at a battered Chris and says, "I mean, I told you not to go in that house." Not only did Chris go in the house, but, just as white people usually do in haunted home narratives, he *stayed*.

Appropriately enough, since many horror films reflect current social or cultural issues, *Get Out* satirizes the supposed "postracial" quality of the twenty-first-century United States. However, it does so in an atypical way. The film is not about a family of racists who try to harm a Black man—quite the opposite, in fact, as the Armitage family prides itself on being above racism, totally unaware of the countless ways they remind Chris that he is different. Rather, the film examines the systemic racism perpetuated by a supposedly liberal family, as well as the persistent ways these liberal white Americans appropriate Black bodies and Black culture.

Get Out was written during Barack Obama's presidency, and Peele wanted to point out "the insidious qualities that white liberals have," as well as the fact that "racism is a human problem," even among those who consider themselves above it. The "sunken place" where the African American targets are exiled while hypnotized by Missy and post-lobotomy is a metaphor for a "state of marginalization," explains Peele. It is "the dark hole we throw black people in," he continues, such as "the prison-industrial complex." It is a place of powerlessness. The "sunken place" also refers to the movie theaters where Black people go to watch horror movies but where they do not see themselves: "We can scream at the screen, but we're not going to get represented on the other side" (qtd. in Lopez). Not only is *Get Out* a commentary on the insidious racism thriving throughout US culture, but it is also a direct statement on the whiteness of horror movies, specifically.

Peele also attributes inspiration to *The Stepford Wives* (Bryan Forbes, 1975), a film that skewered the all-too-perfect behavior of American housewives. In the movie, Joanna Eberhart (Katharine Ross) moves out to the Connecticut suburb of Stepford with her family, only to discover that she has nothing in common with the other housewives, who are all strangely submissive and domes-ticated, even robotic. Joanna eventually discovers that the Stepford housewives have, in fact, literally been replaced with smiling robots, much as Chris discovers that the African Americans he meets through the Armitage fam-ily have literally had their brains removed. Not only was Peele fascinated with the fact that Joanna, much like

Chris, is so reluctant to leave, but he was also drawn to the film's portrayal of the microaggressions that outsiders often experience. As Peele puts it, what *The Stepford Wives* did for gender, *Get Out* does for race (qtd. in Lane).

This is precisely why it is so significant that Chris survives in *Get Out*. Not only is fear a privilege commonly reserved for white people, but surviving that fear is an even bigger privilege. In movie after movie, book after book, African Americans are expendable, inevitable losses on the white hero's journey. So it is meaningful not only that Chris survives—unlike, for instance, the Black protagonist at the heart of *Night of the Living Dead* (George Romero, 1968), who is mercilessly executed despite the fact that he is clearly not a zombie—but that Chris remains at the heart of the narrative. Chris's character has a privilege normally reserved for white protagonists: an emotional narrative arc.

Despite the persistent depiction of horror films as misogynistic, they repeatedly feature the character that Carol Clover describes as the "final girl." While women may be abused and terrorized throughout horror narratives, it is repeatedly the lead female character who takes down her abuser and, significantly, who survives, which complicates our understanding of the misogyny present in so many horror narratives. However, there is no final-girl equivalent with regard to the African American experience. African Americans are either absent entirely or sacrificed (literally or metaphorically) along the way. In *Get Out*, Peele not only shifts this paradigm but makes direct reference to it. After all, what the Armitage family does is silence the voices and ideas and opinions of Black people. The whole premise of the "Sunken Place" is that those voices and ideas and opinions are submerged, concealed, and/or oppressed. By escaping both the "Sunken Place" and the Armitage house, Chris becomes the final girl of sorts, his voice the last one standing.

The film *A House Is Not a Home* (Christopher Ray, 2015) is one of the rare haunted house narratives to include an African American family defending themselves and their home without being a satire. Ben and Linda Williams (played by Gerald Webb and Diahnna Nicole Baxter) buy a new house, hoping that a change of scenery will improve their struggling marriage, that classic idea that a new home will fix things. Linda is trying to leave behind a drinking problem, while Ben is trying to put an affair behind him. Unfortunately for them and their marriage, the house is haunted.

As the youngest and most vulnerable members of the family, the children are the first to realize that the family is under threat. Daughter Ashley Williams (Aurora Perrineau) even tells her parents, "If you cared about us, we would leave." But they do not. The parents continue to be in denial about the spooky events happening in the house, even after a visit from Lucas St. Michelle (Eddie Steeples), a voodoo exorcist. The fact that he practices voodoo, unlike the traditional Catholic priest who is seemingly on speed dial in so many other haunted house narratives, is a fairly distinctive feature, one also seen in *Malicious* (Michael Winnick, 2018).

Gerald Webb, who in addition to playing the male protagonist was also a producer of *A House Is Not a Home*, says that the people involved with the film knew exactly what they were doing in filling a void. He knew they were "breaking new ground for diversity in horror films" and that they specifically wanted to do so "without making [the film] a comedy or insulting stereotypical African-Americans." Webb goes on to point out how shameful it is that "there have historically been very few African-American based horror, occult, and haunted house films produced and distributed." One of the primary goals of the project was to "service the African-American market," allowing Black people finally to see people who looked like them "in the types of horror films that they've long supported." Unfortunately, the film did not start a trend.

Significantly, in *A House Is Not a Home*, the protagonists are not victorious over the evil spirit. There is no resolution. The sign that our protagonists have not won, that good has not triumphed over evil, is revealed at the very end of the film, when Ben's eyes change color, shifting from brown to blue. Webb mentions that, during an early screening of the film, when Lucas first arrives, audience members laughed at his appearance. But as the film progressed, they realized that the cold blue of his eyes represents "his connection and experience with a different and darker spiritual realm" and that they reflect his "multiple encounters with death and evil and the knowledge and abilities he obtained from those encounters to help others," explains Webb. Fundamentally, however, blue eyes have traditionally been seen as a sign of evil, with the ancient Greek philosopher Plutarch arguing that blue-eyed people were usually more powerful at bestowing the curse of the evil eye. So for Ben's eyes to turn blue represents his failure to escape the house, if not also his connection to a darker realm.

Webb points out the difficulties experienced by the film's production team while searching for a distributer, difficulties that point to how unusual a film it is and also to Hollywood's inability to conceptualize a haunted house with Black inhabitants. Countless distributors passed on the film, with reasons varying from "it wouldn't sell overseas" to "we don't know how to market this." As Webb emphasizes, "the distributors we encountered had never seen nor tried to sell a movie like this before and frankly weren't motivated to try." With the recent success of Peele's *Get Out* and his subsequent film *Us* (2019), perhaps distributors will stop feeling as daunted, but as of 2020, there is no sign of significant change.

At first glance, *The Haunted Mansion* (Rob Minkoff, 2003) is a comedic take on the haunted home narrative, complete with all the familiar twists but in a kid-friendly format, as a haunted house movie based on a theme-park attraction should be. However, a closer look reveals a deeply troubling film that, even though it features an African American family in a haunted home, serves more to reinforce the white status quo of both US suburbs and horror films.

One of the first signs that there is something different about this movie is that the Evers family (father Jim, played by Eddie Murphy; mother Sara, played by Marsha Thomason; daughter Megan, played by Aree Davis; and son Michael, played by Marc John Jefferies) does not own the haunted house within which the film takes place. Rather, Jim and Sara are real estate agents who initially come to see the house believing that the owner wants to sell it. In effect, they are in the home as potential employees of the owner. While that is already a significant diversion from the norm, it turns out that that story was just a ruse to bring Sara to the house. Why was Sara brought to the house? Because the house's original owner, Master

Gracey (Nathaniel Parker), wants to marry her. Sara's own particular preference (to stay married to her actual husband) is irrelevant, and the last act of the movie is devoted to Master Gracey and his butler, Ramsley (Terence Stamp), fighting with Jim over ownership of Sara, as if she were a particularly nice piece of furniture.

The backstory lends yet another wrinkle to the film's supposed comedic take. It turns out that Master Gracey is determined to marry Sara because she looks exactly like a woman named Elizabeth with whom he had been desperately in love back in the eighteenth century. However, their love went unrequited because Elizabeth was an African American servant in his household and he was a white wealthy land owner. Despite the fact that Gracey does not care and is willing to do anything to marry his love, the family butler refuses to allow such a transgression and personally kills Elizabeth. To make matters worse, Ramsley makes the death appear to be a suicide, faking a suicide note to Gracey, which throws Gracey into such a depression that he kills himself, cursing the mansion forever and trapping hundreds of ghostly spirits inside.

Spotting Sara's face on a real estate ad and immediately noticing the resemblance, Ramsley concocts the plan to bring Sara to the mansion, believing that if Sara dies, he can bring Sara's ghost and Gracey's ghost together, and the curse will be lifted. Unfortunately for Ramsley, despite offering strict instructions for Sara to come alone, she arrives with her family. Her husband is especially excited about the potential listing, a detail that fits in with his personality as a bad husband and father: he is perpetually choosing work responsibility over family.

Another sign that this is not an ordinary haunted house tale is that the Everses are not the central characters. Rather, they are supporting characters to those who live in the actual mansion: Gracey, Ramsley, and servants Ezer (Wallace Shawn) and Emma (Dina Waters), as well as Madame Leota (Jennifer Tilly), whose head offers wisdom from within a crystal ball. The Everses are there to liberate those characters, as well as the hundreds of others in the cemetery out back. Yet another twist is that, once the Everses have succeeded in helping those characters "find the light," as Emma puts it, they are gifted the home. So, unlike every other haunted home narrative, the family gets the home at the very end of the film, rather than as the inciting incident, and, significantly, the house is *given* to them, rather than their having the agency and clout to buy it.

This is a running gag, in fact. Jim Evers, ambitious real estate agent, is hopelessly uncouth and out of place within the mansion. When Jim asks Ramsley about important qualifications for the position of butler, just in case Evers needs to hire one—an option that seems unlikely at best—Ramsley replies, "Attention to detail, understanding priorities," and after a pause, "knowing one's place." The implication is that Evers does not know *his* place, a cruel comment often directed at African Americans. Later, Ramsley even describes Evers as an "insufferable fool."

While it is not surprising that Evers is the last member to acknowledge the supernatural presence in the Gracey mansion, the film also makes a point of emphasizing how timid and ineffectual both Evers and his young son, Michael, are. Early in the film, both Evers and Michael are unable to kill a spider. Impatient, daughter Megan stomps into the room and takes care of the spider herself. This theme is repeated throughout the movie. Evers and Michael are often afraid or incompetent or both, while Megan has no problem tackling ghosts and other problems head-on. Evers, in contrast, cannot wait to leave the house (perhaps a subtle reference to Murphy's stand-up routine) and fails over and over at his attempts to save his family. He even declares, near the end of the movie, when his focus should be on saving his wife, "I'm feeling fragile right now," and has to be urged by other characters not to give up. Not only does the film reinforce the notion of females as responsible for cleaning up the domestic arena, but it also paints a scathing portrayal of the African American male.

SATIRE AS SOCIAL COMMENTARY

Until African American horror movies become more commonplace, satire remains one of the few opportunities to call attention not only to the lack of racial representation in haunted house narratives but also to the insidious habit of viewing whiteness as neutral, as a default. As Richard Dyer argues, "white power secures its dominance by seeming not to be anything in particular" (44). One of the most useful attributes of comedic takes on horror tropes is precisely their ability to question that which we consider to be "the norm," not only questioning the prevalence of whiteness but also questioning common behaviors and patterns within these narratives. Another benefit, of course, is the appearance (however fleeting) of racial diversity on-screen!

While *Scary Movie* (Keenan Ivory Wayans, 2000) primarily skewers the films *Scream* (Wes Craven, 1996) and *Scream 2* (Wes Craven, 1997), *Scary Movie 2* (Keenan Ivory Wayans, 2001) specifically parodies the tropes of haunted house narratives, making direct reference to films such as *The Legend of Hell House* (John Hough, 1973), *The Amityville Horror* (Stuart Rosenberg, 1979), *The Changeling* (Peter Medak, 1980), *Poltergeist,* and *The Haunting* (Jan de Bont, 1999). The premise of *Scary Movie 2* is straightforward and familiar: Professor Oldman (Tim

Curry) and his assistant, Dwight Hartman (David Cross), want to study potential paranormal activity at a supposedly haunted mansion. Selecting several undergraduates to help them with their research, the professor and his assistant set up camp in the house, somewhat supervised by the caretaker Hanson (Chris Elliot). Suffice to say, the house is haunted, and despite the hijinks and the clichéd plot points, the film is most useful as a commentary on the whiteness of haunted house narratives and the absurdity of the horror genre's most common tropes.

Scary Movie 2 verbalizes that otherwise-unspoken question: Why do white people act the way they do when they see a ghost? For instance, Brenda (Regina Hall) asks, "How come every time some scary shit happens, you white people say, 'Let's split up'?" Despite the fact that she insists that the group should stick together—defying stereotype and expectation—the characters split up anyway, rendering them more vulnerable to attack. At another point, Cindy (Anna Farris), who could not be more white or more blond, runs screaming from a skeleton, to which Brenda, bemused, says, it is "just a skeleton."

Similarly, in *A Haunted House* (Michael Tiddes, 2013), Kisha (Essence Atkins) moves in to her boyfriend Malcolm's (Marlon Wayans) home. In a reference to found-footage horror films such as *Paranormal Activity*

(Oren Peli, 2007)—in which a young couple record supernatural activity in their new home—Malcolm sets up video cameras in the house to prove to Kisha that the house is not haunted. As soon as Malcolm figures out that the house is, indeed, haunted, his first instinct is to leave: "This is for white people. This ain't what n——s do. We don't investigate. We run. We run. We live." The film repeatedly distinguishes between the way white people and Black people react to evil spirits. Marlon Wayans, who also wrote and produced the movie along with his writing partner Rick Alvarez, argues that the film is not a typical parody. Rather, it attempts to show how a Black couple would react to a situation we have seen time and time again with white protagonists (Hailey).

A HELPING HAND

Despite the overwhelming whiteness of families in haunted home narratives, there are a few in which an African American character comes in to save the day. Provided the Black actor is not the hero of the film, it does not upset tradition too much to bring him in to offer advice. Not only is it often the case that outsiders offer better perspectives, but it seems fitting that the character seen as the "exotic other" would have a special connection to the world of the supernatural.

For instance, in *Malicious*, it feels appropriate to have Delroy Lindo playing the role of Dr. Clark, an expert in voodoo and the paranormal. Who better? Not only is Clark African American—already a stark contrast to the white characters in almost every haunted home narrative—but his otherness is exaggerated by his ghostly blue eyes that do not see "real life" but only the paranormal. His blue eyes, much like Lucas's blue eyes in *A House Is Not a Home*, reflect his connection to the spiritual realm. It seems almost clichéd that Clark has a natural affinity for the paranormal, setting up equipment especially designed to listen to alternate realities as he tries to help Adam and Lisa with the evil spirits haunting their home.

Another Black actor standing out in a sea of whiteness is Erik La Ray Harvey as Devin Pyles in *The Charnel House* (Craig Moss, 2016). Pyles is not just an ordinary tenant of the building. He is also not just the only Black tenant in the building. His father had worked in the slaughterhouse that has now been renovated into the luxury lofts. Pyles introduces himself to Alex Reaves, the owner of the luxury-loft building, as a former military man currently working in intelligence. What Pyles does not reveal is that he is actually there to research the horrific history of the building, including the murders that took place there and the disappearance of a young boy. While Alex denies the strange events that start taking place, Pyles become a confidant for Alex's wife, Charlotte (Nadine Velazquez)—ironically the two people least likely to be believed—and the two of them begin investigating together. Pyles is also the one who ends up putting the pieces together and saving both Charlotte and her daughter, Mia (Makenzie Moss). Much like Clark in *Malicious*, Pyles sees the truth that eludes Alex and the others, partly because of his outsider status but also because of his connection to his father, someone who (it seems) could be killed without causing too much of a stir.

While not involving Black characters, there is a similar dynamic at play in the film *The Curse of La Llorona* (Michael Chaves, 2019), which uses Mexican folklore to add some exotic thrills to an otherwise pedestrian horror film. In the film, Anna (Linda Cardellini) must save her two children from an evil spirit known as La Llorona (Weeping Woman) that is determined to take them as her own. Desperate, Anna enlists the help of a variety of Latin American characters (Tony Amendola as Father Perez and Raymond Cruz as Rafael Olvera), in order to remove this curse from her family. While the premise is different, the victimized family in *The Darkness* (Greg McLean, 2016) also relies on the help of Latin American mystics (Alma Martinez as Teresa and Ilza Ponko as her daughter, Gloria) to restore them back to white normality.

BURIAL GROUNDS

Another way "exotic supernatural forces" show up in haunted home narratives is through their proximity to buried bodies. Not only do haunted home stories often depict poorly buried trauma metaphorically, but they also depict poorly buried trauma literally, cathartic in their appeal but also revealing for their significance. For instance, as Eden Arielle Gordon writes, "By painting Native Americans as supernatural, monolithic entities that torment innocent white families," these horror movies affirm the idea that whiteness is "a 'standard' that is disrupted or haunted by otherness." In Jay Anson's original Amityville novel, a supposedly factual account based on the experiences of George and Katy Lutz and their three children, the couple discover that the Shinnecock Indians had used land on the Amityville River "as an enclosure for the sick, mad, and dying," who were "penned up until they died of exposure." Laughably, Anson goes on to explain that, in the late 1600s, these Indians were "eased" out of the area by American settlers (122). While it seems unlikely that white settlers "eased" Indians out of any area, it is even more unlikely that any element of Anson's story is true, since the Shinnecock Indians lived nowhere near Amityville. Hans Holzer, a professor of paranormal psychology, similarly claims in his book *Murder in Amityville* that Ronald DeFeo, who had committed the original murders that inspired the book and film versions of *The Amityville Horror*, had been possessed by an Indian chief buried at that location.

Native American spirits factor into the mythology behind *The Darkness*, which depicts an average American family with the misfortune to bring an evil force back to their suburban home after a trip to the Grand Canyon. The younger child, Mikey (David Mazouz)—who is also autistic, thus making him more susceptible to supernatural powers—takes some sacred rocks from a spiritual site he stumbles on while exploring. (The implicit message, of course, is that his parents are really to blame for not keeping a closer eye on their child.) This triggers the release of evil forces that affect every member of the family, accentuating their negative characteristics and intensifying conflict. Mikey's mother, Bronny (Radha Mitchell), searches online for an explanation and finds links to Native American mythology. In one of Bronny's internet searches, she finds a website devoted to the "Anasazi Indians," describing them as an ancient civilization "with a rich mythology and complex society" that believed in "powerful demons and supernatural animal spirits." It turns out that the rocks that Mikey took are connected to the mythology of the Anasazi Indians, who believed the disruption of the rocks would release demons. By bringing the rocks back to their suburban home, Mikey also brought back supernatural Native American forces.

In the film *Summer of 84* (François Simard, Anouk Whissell, and Yoann-Karl Whissell, 2018), Davey Armstrong (Graham Verchere), the resident conspiracy theorist, reminds his friends that their houses were all built on Indian burial grounds, using that to explain a supposed demonic presence in his room. His friend Farraday (Cory Gruter-Andrew), accustomed to Davey's flights of fancy, dismisses him, pointing out that there is "literally no proof of that," but David insists that yes, there is. None, however, is offered. In Stephen King's novel *The Shining* (published in 1977 and adapted into a film by Stanley Kubrick in 1980), the hotel is built on an Indian burial ground. An Indian burial ground plays an important role in another of King's novels, *Pet Sematary*, as well as on television shows as varied as *South Park* and *The Simpsons*, where it is used for comedic effect. Even *It: Chapter Two* (Andrés Muschietti, 2019) integrates a Native American ritual into its plot. Since the United States lacks the castles and history that Europe incorporated into its Gothic storytelling, one could argue that part of the appeal of the Native American burial ground (however fictitious) is the magic and mysticism it provides to a relatively young country, as well as reflecting fears that Native Americans will return from the dead to avenge their treatment at the hands of white settlers.

Similar in theme to the haunted home narrative but without the actual haunted house, *Pet Sematary* plays up the dissonance between a beautiful rural community and the horror that lurks within it. There is also the theme of trauma and loss—Rachel mourning her sister, for whose death she feels responsible; Louis, blaming himself for being unable to save a student hit by a car; and then the two of them trying to cope with the death of their son. When their cat is killed, neither parent can tell their daughter, Ellie, what actually happened, choosing instead to lie that the cat must have run away. Because both Rachel and Louis cannot deal with grief, they repress it, and this guarantees that it will return tenfold.

Another aspect of repressed and unresolved grief is tied to the history of the physical location of the cemetery. *Pet Sematary* and the subsequent film adaptations make reference to the Native Americans who had originally lived on land near Louis and Rachel's new home, using the aspect of haunted land to explain why the Native Americans had left. This conveniently erases the actual narrative that white settlers had driven the Native Americans off their land. This intentional omission is particularly relevant since, as King, a Maine resident, was writing *Pet Sematary*, there had been a legal battle between the state of Maine and several Native American tribes that argued that about 60 percent of state land actually belonged to them. Maine eventually had to award the tribes more than $81 million so that existing non-Native Americans would not have to relocate. Land dispute also shows up in *Pet Sematary*, with Native Americans arguing with the state of Maine, as well as with the federal government, over who owns the land.

This question of ownership—not only who owns the land but how this is determined and then, in turn, respected—has proved compelling both in real life and in fictitious narratives, especially with regard to burial sites. Native American burial sites that had been left undisturbed for thousands of years became vulnerable during the eighteenth and nineteenth centuries and only became more vulnerable as US cities and towns grew exponentially. New developments frequently expanded right onto the burial sites, which were either plowed over or picked apart, the bodies themselves unceremoniously removed. For instance, Indian burial sites in Nashville, Tennessee; Canton, Georgia; Oxford, Alabama; Fenton, Montana; and Anderson, California, were all disturbed, with bodies and artifacts moved or just put in storage, to make way for new Walmart buildings, and Walmart is only one of many corporations known for its repeated involvement in the destruction of culturally important Native American sites. The fact that traditionally many Native Americans not only worship at the graves of their ancestors but believe that desecrating these graves will bring harm to the living does not provide enough of a deterrent for many American developers.

In the episode "Open House" of the show *American Horror Story: Murder House* (FX, November 16, 2011), Constance Langdon (Jessica Lange) tells a real estate developer, "Every time you put up one of these monstrous temples to the gods of travertine, you're building on top of someone else's life." His reply? "I'm a developer. I improved on the past." Constance's retort is, simply, "You should show some respect. You're not an archaeologist. You should stop unearthing while you're ahead. It only brings a haunting. We have a responsibility as caretakers to the old lands to show some respect." Only in these narratives, the old lands never receive respect, people rarely act as caretakers, and that same real estate developer (like many others) has no intention of changing his business model.

Other haunted home films, like *Poltergeist*, also feature houses built on burial grounds, even if not necessarily Native American. In *Poltergeist*, the Freeling family lives in a new cookie-cutter suburban development, where Steve (Craig T. Nelson) works as a real estate developer and Diane (JoBeth Williams) takes care of their three children. Creepy events begin to happen with increasing frequency, culminating in the disappearance of their daughter, Carol Anne (Heather O'Rourke). A group of parapsychologists determine that multiple spirits haunt the house, and Steve soon discovers that this is because the house had been built on top of a cemetery. The developer, in order to save money, merely moved the headstones but left the bodies behind in the ground. In the dramatic finale, skeletal corpses surround Diane. When she tries to escape, dragging the children outside to safety, coffins and dead bodies begin emerging from the ground, the desecrated bodies returning to avenge the disrespect with which they were treated. This is a popular motif for haunted home narratives, whether literal or metaphorical, in which the haunting is tied directly to disrespect for the legacy of the home or the land on which it is built.

Similarly, the movie *Grave Secrets: The Legacy of Hilltop Drive* (John Patterson, 1992) features a home built on top of a burial ground, only in this case the burial ground is for African Americans, one of the few times African American history is even acknowledged in haunted house narratives. Like the original *Amityville* book, this film is supposedly based on fact. The story revolves around Jean Williams (Patty Duke) and her husband, Shag Williams (David Selby), who purchase a home in a new housing development, only to discover that the developers built above an old graveyard, as in *Poltergeist*. Even though the developers try to deny this, strange things keep happening until the Williamses fear for their lives. Eventually, the truth comes to light as the ghosts wreak havoc on the community.

In *The House by the Cemetery* (Lucio Fulci, 1981), the Boyle family moves from New York to a small town outside Boston where Norman Boyle (Paolo Malco) intends to complete research begun by his recently deceased colleague, Dr. Petersen. The family moves into the same house where Petersen had killed his mistress before then killing himself. Not only is the house, quite literally, by a cemetery, with tombstones also on the actual property, but there are also tombstones in the house—and Petersen's killings were only a fraction of the murders that took place in that house. Needless to say, evil events transpire as a result. By examining the ways homes—and specifically haunted homes—are portrayed on big and small screens, it is possible to gain a deeper understanding of the impact suburbia has had on Americans. Conversely, by examining the history of suburbia and its sprawling impact on gender roles, racism, family dynamics, and financial instability, it is possible to gain a deeper appreciation of the familiar tale of the haunted home.

THE STATUS QUO

While the lack of racial diversity in haunted home narratives might make it strange to have a chapter devoted
to race in this context, it is precisely because of that lack
that this chapter (and this topic) is important. It is by
calling attention to that lack that we can reach a deeper
understanding of the nefarious impact of so many years
of government-condoned (and government-subsidized)
discriminatory practices, and it is specifically within the
context of haunted homes that we can do so here.

Aviva Briefel and Sianne Ngai, in their article about
the film *Candyman*, quote Douglas Kellner, who argues
that "post-1960 horror films . . . have presented, often
in symbolic/allegorical form, both universal fears and
the deepest anxieties and hostilities of contemporary
U.S. society" (72). Briefel and Ngai, however, write that
despite Kellner's implication that these films focus their
attention on the way the world has changed as a result of
turmoil created by economic crisis, social and cultural
change, and political unrest, they believe that the true
anxiety expressed in these films has to do with spaces
resistant to change: "namely, white, middle-class envi-
ronments" (72). They point out that, while the "fear-
provoking figures vary in appearance from film to film,"
the protagonists resemble one another with their white,

working-to-middle class, heteronormativity, perhaps consciously or subconsciously responding to fears of a diversifying suburbia (73). Jonathan Allen, in an analysis for NBC News, explains comments made by President Donald Trump in a press conference in July 2020; Trump claimed that his opponent in the upcoming election, Joe Biden, wants to "abolish the suburbs." Allen quotes the Democratic strategist Michael Starr Hopkins, who argues that Trump's message is clear: "Elect me and I'll keep Black people out of your neighborhoods and out of your schools." This adherence to a white status quo further reinforces the supposed exclusivity of US suburbs.

Racism in the United States has long been loud and public. But racism in the United States has also been quiet and insidious, lurking behind government policy, corporate bureaucracy, and Hollywood's casting choices. While haunted home narratives are not generally considered political statements, perhaps they speak loudly for what is absent, demonstrating the persistent whiteness of US suburbs and US horror films, schemes that were decades in the making.

CONCLUSION

The same period of time marked by the proliferation of US suburbs—the mid-1940s through the early 1970s—was also marked by the proliferation of another concept: "late capitalism." First coined by the German economist Werner Sombart at the start of the twentieth century, the term was popularized by the Marxist economist Ernest Mandel to describe the increasing industrialization of human life, the rise of the multinational corporation and a globalized economy, and the massive explosion of capitalism, production, and consumption that marked the years after World War II. In 1984, Fredric Jameson added another layer to the concept—that life would, as a result of the changes laid out by Mandel, become progressively commodified and disposable. More recently, Annie Lowrey writes that late capitalism now connotes the breakdown of the US economic promise, exposing the growing disparity between the very rich and the very poor, the way government policy favors some and punishes others. She quotes Mike Konczal, a fellow at the Roosevelt Institute, who links late capitalism to the financial crisis of 2008 and the subsequent decade, arguing that the two "stripped away a veneer on what's going on in the economy."

The concept of late capitalism, and its various implications, provides an apt reflection not only of shifts in the US economy but shifts in suburbia, as well. From the years directly following World War II through to the present day, the American dream, much like the American suburb, has been manipulated (for better and for worse) by extensive government policy, fostered by a veritable orgy of capitalistic consumption (buy a car! buy a dishwasher! buy a television! buy three!) and fueled by the racial, economic, and gendered disparity at its core.

Another impact of late capitalism is the emphasis placed on streamlining individuality and maximizing profit. While these priorities are hardly new—see the original Levittown developments, for example—the domestic space, much like the workplace, has become more clearly about function and efficiency rather than nurturing personal growth. In the interests of efficiency and profit margins, the default aesthetic is likely to be cold and minimal, with glass walls, windows, and stark, rectangular rooms. And within those rooms? The unrelenting integration of technology—voice controlled, motion sensitive, and fully automated. This integration has had an impact not only on the porous nature of public-versus-private space but also on how humans exist within their own homes.

Tyson Lewis and Daniel Cho, in their article "Home Is Where the Neurosis Is: A Topography of the Spatial Unconscious," address the infiltration of technology into everyday life, writing that "the private internal space previously reserved for contemplation and development [is] now consumed by dehumanizing devices" (75). Not only has the basic concept of privacy been dramatically overhauled over the past two decades (if not eradicated), but private personal space, that space in which we should feel most human, has been consumed by tools that encourage the opposite.

We can see this dynamic play out in Oren Peli's film *Paranormal Activity* (2007), in which technology is used to document the supernatural forces haunting the home belonging to Katie (Katie Featherston) and Micah (Micah Sloat). Through a camera that Micah sets up in their bedroom (the room that should be the most private and personal), the couple are able to see and hear disturbing events, including demonic grunting, Katie in a trance, and unexplained movement by various objects. Eventually the supernatural forces take possession of Katie, who kills Micah, as seen via found footage. The found footage is so integral to the story's narrative that it would be impossible to imagine one without the other. Appropriately enough, "found-footage documentation" also plays a pivotal role in the subsequent *Paranormal Activity* films. Similarly, the reality television show *Ghost Hunters*, which aired on the SciFi Channel (2004–9), Syfy (2009–16), and A&E (2019–present), uses technology to detect paranormal activity. Much like in *Rose Red*, the team members set up electronic equipment to search for paranormal activity, including taking electromagnetic-field readings, monitoring the room's temperature, recording audio, and filming the supposedly haunted site. Our homes, our private spaces, are consumed by dehumanizing devices searching for answers.

The infiltration of technology erodes not only boundaries between public and private but also those between past and present. Technology blends both time and space, making everything appear to be "now" and "nearby." This further intertwines the past with the present, ensuring that the future comes complete with plenty of residual baggage, literalizing the blurring of timelines seen in movies such as *The Haunting of Hill House* (Mike Flanagan, 2018).

A remake of the Japanese horror film *Ringu* (Hideo Nakata, 1998), *The Ring* (Gore Verbinski, 2002) stars Naomi Watts as a journalist researching a videotape that causes the subsequent death of anyone who watches it. A critical and commercial success, *The Ring* not only spawned two sequels, as well as encouraging subsequent English-language remakes of countless other Asian horror films, but also serves as an interesting reflection on how technology has been integrated into horror movies. Eric White, writing on *Ringu*, argues that the film "associates ubiquitous technological mediation—that is, the cameras, television sets, videocassette recorders, telephones, and other such hardware foregrounded through the film—with the intrusion of 'posthuman' otherness into contemporary cultural life" (41). Otherness now rides in on wireless frequencies.

Not only does watching the videotape trigger a series of events ending in death for characters in *The Ring*, but the footage on the videotape is a recorded version of visions that might appear in more traditional haunted home films. Whereas once these images might have appeared in mirrors or in dreams, in this film the striking and ominous images appear on television screens. Exactly as in traditional haunted home films, the images on the videotape reflect unresolved trauma by those souls unable to leave the mortal plane. When Rachel, for instance, holds the tape out to Richard Morgan (Brian Cox), she says, "I think it's a message from your wife." It is unclear, however, if it is a message from his wife or from his daughter, both long deceased under traumatic circumstances, with lots of unresolved issues.

The film makes a point of blurring the line between the two- and three-dimensional, making it clear that the horrific images are not neatly confined to a monitor. Much like in traditional haunted home films, in which ghosts can cause physical disruption to space and bodies, the central characters in *The Ring* end up acquiring bruises in the imprint of clenched hands, similar to those of Carolyn Perron (Lili Taylor) in *The Conjuring* (James Wan, 2013). Another way of blurring the two worlds occurs when images from the videotape playing on a monitor become physical, entering the world in which the monitor itself exists. In one scene, for instance, Rachel (Naomi Watts) plucks a fly that had been within the recorded images off the actual television monitor on which the footage is playing. It is now a three-dimensional creature. Even more dramatically, the evil spirit itself crawls out of the television to kill Noah Clay (Martin Henderson). Significantly, back in 1982, in Tobe Hooper's *Poltergeist*, the television set only sucks victims in. It does not send evil spirits *out*.

In *The Ring*, the television set is a conduit between other worlds and our reality. Throughout the film, televisions communicate with "staticky blurts" (as described in the subtitles), hinting at an evil presence. Similarly,

Noah says that Samara (Daveigh Chase) was "not alone" when they find the alcove where she was confined, because she was confined with a television set. In 2020, the notion of interacting with your television set, with speaking to a video-beamed face that responds, is far from crazy. It is actually quite normal. With your smartphone, you never feel alone.

This concept is central to the film *Pulse* (Jim Sonzero, 2006), another English-language remake of an Asian horror film, Kiyoshi Kurosawa's *Kairo* (2001). In *Pulse*, the threat is far more interactive and aggressive than in *The Ring*. Playing on our fondness for internet-based communication, evil forces communicate via online messages, even when the computer is unplugged or turned off, as well as via cell phones and other handheld wireless devices. Much as televisions are seemingly ubiquitous in *The Ring*, in this film, phones and computers appear everywhere. The terrifying characters who show up on computer monitors also show up on reflective surfaces such as mirrors and windows. They do not, interestingly, travel via television frequencies, seemingly preferring Wi-Fi.

The notion that the scary footage is not restricted to a conventional two-dimensional reality is played up when Mattie (Kristen Bell) asks Dex (Ian Somerhalder) how long he has been watching the scary footage. His reply is, "How long have they been watching me?" Technological interactions are far from one-sided. Ghosts, through the computer, ask potential victims if they want to meet a ghost before draining their victims' life force, and they expect an answer. When Mattie unplugs her computer to avoid seeing an image, it just comes through the printer, because ghosts are not easily deterred and because technology has infiltrated all aspects of our lives. There is no way to shut down the evil force because it *is* the actual system now. Josh (Jonathan Tucker) explains that the evil force has gotten loose within the computer network, and now "it's burning through every firewall."

To make things worse, communication networks are virtually everywhere. In other words, every home has been penetrated, and so every home must be abandoned. The only way to protect oneself is by "sealing a room," which entails sealing doors and windows and disconnecting the computer, but this only works until you have to step outside. The only way to escape properly is by leaving the cities, going to "dead zones" where technology does not function. However, as we all know, far too few of those dead zones exist.

Much like in *The Ring*, there are echoes of more conventional haunted home narratives within *Pulse*. Mattie, for instance, keeps being told that she is imagining everything. Even when she recognizes that all the suicides are connected, Dex tells her that he is not buying it and that the idea of ghosts traveling through Wi-Fi makes no sense. But what makes this narrative far more chilling is that, as a result of technology, there is no escape, even when Dex finally admits that Mattie is right.

The premise behind *The Charnel House* (Craig Moss, 2016) is that Alex Reaves (Callum Blue), with the assistance of his wife, Charlotte (Nadine Velazquez), converts an abandoned slaughterhouse into a luxury apartment building complete with state-of-the-art technology. As Alex himself describes it, "the entire building is automated," which means that the residents "can control everything": "the doors, the lights, the showers," even coffee machines and garbage disposals. Jackson (Andy Favreau) describes it as "the home of the future," to which Alex replies, "This is the home of your present."

The technology regulates temperatures, lights, visuals, and sounds. However, what this means is that everything *needs* to be controlled using technology, which, in effect, means that technology controls everything. Alex argues that all the automation is designed to keep residents "zen-like, happy, and content." However, it really just strips them of agency. You cannot open a door unless the building permits you to do so. And the building will open (and close) the door at its desired speed.

Unfortunately, not only was the building originally a slaughterhouse for cows, but it was also the site of many murders, the bodies ground up and concealed within the meat. Alex does not tell his wife that people had been murdered in the slaughterhouse because he "didn't think it was relevant" and because it happened "a long time ago." In familiar fashion, he insists that what happened was "in the past" and should have no bearing on the future he is building for the family. When she continues to press him, he defensively implies that she should have known something had happened in the building, that there had to have been "some kind of issues," because how else could they have afforded to buy it?

While this is all typical to haunted home narratives in general, what is uniquely contemporary is the way the evil forces communicate with the building's residents. The technology facilitates communication for the evil forces in the house, acting as a conduit, much like in *The Ring* and *Pulse*. The evil forces take over the screens installed throughout the complex, communicating with images as well as with text. For instance, they depict horrific images from the building's past, such as cows screaming in pain, carcasses, body parts, and skeletons, as well as messages simply stating, "I want you to die," directed at specific tenants. Devin Pyles (Erik LaRay Harvey) even sees the murder of his father play out on a monitor.

Just like in *The Ring*, the images also become three-dimensional, blood literally dripping off the monitor.

Blaine Cornish (Neil Thackaberry), a local historian, tells Alex, "I can only imagine the horrors you've found buried inside this awful building." However, when the evil forces turn on Alex, he sees the horrors firsthand on the building's monitors and then experiences them directly in the building's basement, unable to escape because the building will not unlock its doors. This makes it clear that the horrors are not confined to the two-dimensional plane. The evil forces also turn on Emily Turner (Danielle Lauder), triggering the garbage disposal when she is bending over her kitchen sink, sucking her hair and directly leading to her death. After she dies, the evil forces text Jackson via monitor in her stead.

When Devin asks Mia (Makenzie Moss) where Rupert (Alden Tab) went, Mia points to a monitor and says, "He's in there." A ghostly presence, the childlike Rupert routinely communicates via screens, appearing within them and addressing Mia directly. Much like in traditional haunted home narratives, Charlotte repeatedly tells her daughter to stop imagining things, that she needs to learn to distinguish between "imagination and reality," but just like in those narratives, Mia turns out to be right about Rupert. Rupert exists, and his presence has consequences.

The film's big reveal is that Alex is actually Rupert or at least part of him. During a traumatic event in Rupert's childhood, his soul split from his body and never became reconnected. The implication is that Alex set up the technology in the building where the trauma had occurred to allow the past to communicate with the present, to resolve his body/soul split. He wants "to reconnect," for "his split soul to return here, merge, and die as one like he was supposed to," explains Devin. If anything gets in his way, "both he and this place will work in concert to get rid of them." Alex, Rupert, and the building are all working as one.

The methods may have changed, but the underlying narrative is the same: the domestic space, the realm of the private and safe, is revealed to be as dangerous (if not more dangerous) than the world at large. Boundaries between private and public, as well as boundaries between past and present, are revealed to be porous, data from one flowing into the other, much like the split between Alex and Rupert. In the film *Host* (Rob Savage, 2020), our protagonists are conducting a séance—via Zoom—while under COVID-19 lockdown. Once the séance goes wrong, however, physical location becomes irrelevant. The evil spirit attacks all the women, moving rapidly from one to another as if through the Zoom software itself.

Haunted home narratives, in particular, are well suited to exploring the various ways these boundaries have

eroded, leaving the supposed sanctity of the home vulnerable to electronic signals and devices of every sort. If
anything, technology has rendered us more vulnerable
rather than less. The portals to hell are still there—they
still favor attics and basements—but now they can also
come out of your television or computer monitor. They
do not merely communicate in dreams and visions but
also via text message and email. These shifts reinforce the
idea that haunted homes in US film and television speak
to us not about some archaic past but about our suburban
present, if not also our suburban future.

ACKNOWLEDGMENTS

A special thank you to Nicole Solano of Rutgers University Press and the Quick Takes series editors, Gwendolyn Audrey Foster and Wheeler Winston Dixon, for shepherding this project from a crazy idea to a tangible object. Thank you to Alison Desposito for keeping me embraced as I was working on this occasionally grim project. Thank you to Jude Rawlins for reminding me that not all ideas are garbage, to Tom Schweitzer for keeping my writing respectable, and to Lauren Boumaroun, Ana Julia Ferrer-Jenkins, Andrew Katz, Amanda Reyes, and Mike White for the support. A special thanks to William Mooney and Patrick Knisley for giving me the time to get this finished. As always, I am grateful to Bowie and Franklin for the love.

FURTHER READING

Curtis, Barry. *Dark Places: The Haunted House in Film*. London: Reaktion Books, 2008.

Hayden, Dolores. *Redesigning the American Dream: The Future of Housing, Work, and Family Life*. New York: Norton, 2002.

Jackson, Shirley. *The Haunting of Hill House*. New York: Penguin, 2013.

Matheson, Richard. *Hell House*. New York: Tom Doherty, 1999.

McRoy, Jay, ed. *Japanese Horror Cinema*. Edinburgh: Edinburgh University Press, 2005.

Mumford, Lewis. *The City in History: Its Origins, Its Transformations, and Its Prospects*. San Diego: Harcourt, 1989.

Murphy, Bernice. *The Suburban Gothic in American Popular Culture*. New York: Palgrave Macmillan, 2009.

Nicolaides, Becky M., and Andrew Wiese, eds. *The Suburb Reader*. New York: Routledge, 2006.

Poe, Edgar Allan. "The Fall of the House of Usher." *Thirty-Two Stories*. Ed. Stuart Levine and Susan F. Levine. Indianapolis: Hackett, 2000. 87–103.

Schubart, Rikke. *Mastering Fear: Women, Emotions, and Contemporary Horror*. New York: Bloomsbury Academic, 2018.

Underwood, Tim, and Chuck Miller, eds. *Bare Bones: Conversations on Terror with Stephen King*. New York: Warner, 1989.

Wiese, Andrew. *Places of Their Own: African American Suburbanization in the Twentieth Century*. Chicago: University of Chicago Press, 2004.

Wood, Robin. "Return of the Repressed." *Film Comment* 14.4 (1978): 24–32.

WORKS CITED

Allen, Jonathan. "Five Decades Later, Trump Is Still Pushing
     Segregationist Policies." NBC News 16 July 2020. Web.
     https://www.nbcnews.com/politics/donald-trump/
     five-decades-later-trump-still-pushing-segregationist
     -policies-n1233983.

Anson, Jay. *The Amityville Horror*. New York: Pocket Star
     Books, 2005.

Bloom, Mike. "'The Haunting of Hill House' Creator
     Addresses the Show's Biggest Terrors and Twists."
     Hollywood Reporter 15 Oct. 2018. Web. https://www
     .hollywoodreporter.com/live-feed/haunting-hill-house
     -finale-mike-flanagan-interview-1151590.

Briefel, Aviva, and Sianne Ngai. "'How Much Did You Pay
     for This Place?' Fear, Entitlement, and Urban Space in
     Bernard Rose's *Candyman*." *Camera Obscura* 13.1 (1996):
     69–91. Print.

Cannato, Vincent. "A Home of One's Own." *National Affairs*
     Spring 2010. Web. https://www.nationalaffairs.com/
     publications/detail/a-home-of-ones-own.

Chan, Andrew. "Waking Nightmares: A Conversation with
     Jordan Peele." *Criterion* 23 Feb. 2017. Web. https://www
     .criterion.com/current/posts/4439-waking-nightmares
     -a-conversation-with-jordan-peele.

Church, David. "Return of the Return of the Repressed: Notes on the American Horror Film 1991–2006." *Off Screen* 10.10 (2006). Web. https://offscreen.com/view/return_of_the_repressed.

Clover, Carol. *Men, Women, and Chainsaws*. Princeton, NJ: Princeton UP, 1992. Print.

Curtis, Barry. *Dark Places: The Haunted House in Film*. London: Reaktion Books, 2008. Print.

DePalma, Anthony. "In the Nation: Why Owning a Home Is the American Dream." *New York Times* 11 Sept. 1988. Web. https://www.nytimes.com/1988/09/11/realestate/in-the-nation-why-owning-a-home-is-the-american-dream.html.

Derrida, Jacques. "From *Specters of Marx*." *The Derrida Reader: Writing Performances*. Ed. Julian Wolfreys. Lincoln: University of Nebraska Press, 1998. 140–68. Print.

Dyer, Richard. "White." *Screen* 29.4 (1988): 44–65. Print.

Entertainment Tonight. "Jordan Peele Reveals How Eddie Murphy Inspired 'Get Out.'" YouTube 24 Feb. 2017. Web. https://www.youtube.com/watch?v=i9kwSoO3jUU.

Flood, Alison, "'Textbook Terror': How The Haunting of Hill House Rewrote Horror's Rules." *The Guardian* 11 Oct. 2018. Web. https://www.theguardian.com/books/2018/oct/11/textbook-terror-how-the-haunting-of-hill-house-rewrote-horrors-rules.

Franklin, Ruth. "The Haunting of Hill House Recap: The Sleep of Reason." *Vulture* 17 Oct. 2018. Web. https://www.vulture.com/2018/10/the-haunting-of-hill-house-recap-season-1-episode-9.html.

Friedan, Betty. *The Feminine Mystique*. New York: Norton, 1963. Print.

Frosh, Stephen. *Hauntings: Psychoanalysis and Ghostly Transmissions*. New York: Palgrave Macmillan, 2013. Print.

Glantz, Aaron, and Emmanuel Martinez. "Modern-Day Redlining: How Banks Block People of Color from Homeownership." *Chicago Tribune* 17 Feb. 2018. Web. https://www.chicagotribune.com/business/ct-biz -modern-day-redlining-20180215-story.html.

Gordon, Eden Arielle. "Who's Really Haunting America? Deconstructing the Indian Burial Ground Trope." *Popdust* 3 Aug. 2020. Web. https://www.popdust.com/ indian-burial-ground-trope-2646872020.html.

Guerra, Katherine. "I Never Wanted to Be Your Mother: The Resistant Mother in Millennial Horror Films *The Babadook* and *Hereditary*." Paper presented at the Society of Cinema and Media Studies conference, Seattle, WA, 16 Mar. 2019.

Hailey, Jonathan. "Marlon Wayans: Halloween Is like a Pedophile's Homecoming." *Urban Daily* 23 Oct. 2012. Web. https://theurbandaily.com/1965259/marlon -wayans-a-haunted-house-halloween-richard-pryor -interview/.

Hayden, Dolores. *Redesigning the American Dream: The Future of Housing, Work, and Family Life*. New York: Norton, 2002. Print.

Holzer, Hans. *Murder in Amityville*. New York: Belmont Tower Books, 1979.

Jackson, Shirley. *The Haunting of Hill House*. Faded Page, 2018. eBook.

Jameson, Fredric. "Postmodernism, or The Cultural Logic of Late Capitalism." *New Left Review* 146 (July–Aug. 1984): 53–92. Web. https://newleftreview.org/issues/I146/articles/fredric-jameson-postmodernism-or-the-cultural-logic-of-late-capitalism.

Joho, Jess. "The Witch Isn't an Empowerment Narrative and That's Why It's Great." *Kill Screen* 23 Feb. 2016. Web. https://killscreen.com/previously/articles/the-witch-isnt-an-empowerment-narrative-and-thats-why-its-great/.

Jones, Stephen. *Clive Barker's A–Z of Horror*. New York: Harper Paperbacks, 1998. Print.

Kawash, Samira. "Safe House? Body, Building, and the Question of Security." *Cultural Critique* 45 (2000): 185–221. Print.

King, Stephen. *It*. New York: Scribner, 2017. Print.

———. *Pet Sematary*. New York: Pocket Books, 1983. Print.

———. *The Shining*. New York: Doubleday, 1977. Print.

———. "Terror Ink." *Bare Bones: Conversations on Terror with Stephen King*. Ed. Tim Underwood and Chuck Miller. New York: Warner, 1989. 93–124. Print.

Kit, Borys, "Berlin: Vertical Entertainment Picks Up Horror Movie 'Malicious.'" *Hollywood Reporter* 16 Feb. 2018. Web. https://www.hollywoodreporter.com/heat-vision/malicious-horror-movie-sells-vertical-entertainment-1085377.

Klein, Aaron. Interview with the author. 28 May 2019. Phone.

Knapp, Kathy. "The Business of Forgetting: Postwar Living Memorials and the Post-Traumatic Suburb in Chang-rae Lee's 'Aloft.'" *Twentieth Century Literature* 59.2 (2013): 196–231. Print.

Kruse, Kevin M. *White Flight: Atlanta and the Making of Modern Conservatism*. Princeton, NJ: Princeton UP, 2017. Print.

Lam, Jeff. Message to the author. 3 Apr. 2019. Email.

Lane, Michael. "Living in the Sunken Place: An Analysis of 'Get Out.'" *Jet Fuel Review Blog* 20 Apr. 2018. Web. https://lewislitjournal.wordpress.com/2018/04/20/living-in-the-sunken-place-an-analysis-of-get-out/.

Lewis, Tyson, and Daniel Cho. "Home Is Where the Neurosis Is: A Topography of the Spatial Unconscious." *Cultural Critique* 64 (2006): 69–91. Print.

Lipsitz, George. "The Possessive Investment in Whiteness: Racialized Social Democracy and the 'White' Problem in American Studies." *The Suburb Reader*. Ed. Becky M. Nicolaides and Andrew Wiese. New York: Routledge, 2006. 341–44. Print.

Lopez, Ricardo. "Jordan Peele on How He Tackled Systemic Racism as Horror in 'Get Out.'" *Variety* 1 Nov. 2017. Web. https://variety.com/2017/film/news/jordan-peele-get-out-systemic-racism-1202604824/.

Lowery, Annie. "Why the Phrase 'Late Capitalism' Is Suddenly Everywhere." *Atlantic* 1 May 2017. Web. https://www.theatlantic.com/business/archive/2017/05/late-capitalism/524943/.

Macy, Trevor. Interview with the author. 13 May 2019. Phone.

Mandel, Ernest. *Late Capitalism*. London: Verso, 1978,

Marshall, Colin. "Levittown, the Prototypical American
     Suburb—A History of Cities in 50 Buildings, Day
     25." *The Guardian* 28 Apr. 2015. Web. https://www
     .theguardian.com/cities/2015/apr/28/levittown
     -america-prototypical-suburb-history-cities.

Moloney, Susie. *The Dwelling*. New York: Atria Books, 2003.
     Print.

Morgenson, Gretchen. "Home Loans: A Nightmare Grows
     Darker." *New York Times* 8 Apr. 2007. Web. https://www
     .nytimes.com/2007/04/08/business/yourmoney/
     08gret.html.

Mumford, Lewis. *The City in History: Its Origins, Its Trans-
     formations, and Its Prospects*. San Diego: Harcourt, 1989.
     Print.

Murphy, Bernice. *The Suburban Gothic in American Popular
     Culture*. New York: Palgrave Macmillan, 2009. Print.

Nicolaou, Elena. "Is *The Haunting of Hill House* Based on
     a True Story?" *Refinery29* 9 Oct. 2018. Web. https://
     www.refinery29.com/en-us/2018/10/213244/netflix
     -haunting-of-hill-house-true-story-real-place.

Poe, Edgar Allan. "The Fall of the House of Usher." *Thirty-
     Two Stories*. Ed. Stuart Levine and Susan F. Levine.
     Indianapolis: Hackett, 2000. 87–103. Print.

Rothstein, Richard. *The Color of Law: A Forgotten History
     of How Our Government Segregated America*. New York:
     Liveright, 2017.

———. "A 'Forgotten History' of How the U.S. Government
     Segregated America." Interview by Terry Gross. *Fresh Air*
     (National Public Radio) 3 May 2017. Web. https://www

.npr.org/2017/05/03/526655831/a-forgotten-history-of
-how-the-u-s-government-segregated-america.

Ryan, Hugh. "'The Babadook' Is a Horror Movie about a
Mother Who Hates Her Son." *Vice* 25 Nov. 2014. Web.
https://www.vice.com/en_us/article/yvq4jv/horror
-movie-the-babadook-explores-mothers-who-hate-their
-sons.

Schubart, Rikke. *Mastering Fear: Women, Emotions, and Contemporary Horror.* New York: Bloomsbury Academic,
2018. Print.

Sombart, Werner. *Der Moderne Kapitalismus.* Berlin:
Duncker and Humblot, 1902.

US Census Bureau, Housing and Household Economic Statistics Division. "Historical Census of Housing Tables."
31 Oct. 2011. Web. https://www.census.gov/hhes/www/
housing/census/historic/owner.html.

Vagianos, Alanna. "30 Shocking Domestic Violence
Statistics That Remind Us It's an Epidemic." *Huffington
Post* 23 Oct. 2014, updated 6 Dec. 2017. Web. https://
www.huffpost.com/entry/domestic-violence-statistics
_n_5959776.

Webb, Gerald. Interview with the author. 5 May 2019. Face-
book Messenger.

Whalen, Andrew. "'Haunting of Hill House' Is Based
on Many True Stories." *Newsweek* 15 Oct. 2018. Web.
https://www.newsweek.com/haunting-hill-house
-based-true-story-ghosts-book-shirley-jackson-1171314.

White, Eric. "Case Study: Nakata Hideo's *Ringu* and *Ringu
2.*" *Japanese Horror Cinema.* Ed. Jay McRoy. Edinburgh:
Edinburgh University Press, 2005. 38–47. Print.

Wiese, Andrew. *Places of Their Own: African American Suburbanization in the Twentieth Century*. Chicago: University of Chicago Press, 2004. Print.

Wood, Robin. "Return of the Repressed." *Film Comment* 14.4 (1978): 24–32. Print.

INDEX

Allen, Lewis, 2, 5, 35

American Horror Story: Murder House: and burial sites, 143; and evil spirits, 42–43; and gender, 74–75, 78; and homeownership, 20, 22; and sentient homes, 55

American Poltergeist, 24

Amityville Horror, The (book), 138, 139, 144

Amityville Horror, The (movie): and *Amityville II: The Possession*, 21–22; and basements, 48; and burial grounds, 138–39; and domestic violence, 66–68; and homeownership, 23; and references to, 120, 133

Amityville II: The Possession, 21, 48, 49, 68

Amityville 4: The Evil Escapes, 49, 97

Amityville 6: It's About Time, 49, 97, 109

Annabelle, 103

Annabelle: Creation, 103

Anson, Jay, 138

Aster, Ari, 3, 48, 90, 91

Babadook, The, 5, 36–37, 48, 80

Blatty, William Peter, 77

Briefel, Aviva, 119, 146–47

Burnt Offerings, 48

Byrne, Sean, 25

Candyman, 119, 146

Carpenter, John, 31

Caruso, D. J., 48, 76

Cat and the Canary, The, 2

Changeling, The, 48, 50, 133

Charnel House, The, 48, 71, 136, 156–59

Christine, 31

Clayton, Jack, 4, 208

Color of Law, The: A Forgotten History of How Our Government Segregated America, 116–17

Conjuring, The, 48, 72, 153

Conjuring 2, The, 43

Curse of La Llorona, The, 137

Curtis, Barry, 33

Damiani, Damiano, 21
Darkness, The, 111, 137, 139
Devil's Candy, The, 25–26
Disappointments Room, The, 48, 76, 82, 93
Doctor Sleep, 55
Don't Be Afraid of the Dark, 20, 48, 49, 107–8
Dracula, 29
Dyer, Richard, 133

Eggers, Robert, 4, 100
Entity, The, 65, 72
Exorcist, The (book), 77
Exorcist, The (movie), 102–3

Fair Housing Act, 115
Falchuk, Brad, 20
Fall of the House of Usher, The, 49
Federal Housing Administration (FHA), 11, 13, 115–17
Federal National Mortgage Association (Fannie Mae), 11
Feminine Mystique, The, 62
Flanagan, Mike: and the appeal of horror narratives, 70; and *Doctor Sleep*, 55; and the domestic front, 3; and the economics of homeownership, 21; and lies, 45; and nonlinear narratives, 151; and unresolved trauma, 33, 40, 41, 54

Fodor, Nandor, 42
Frankenstein, 29
Freud, Sigmund, 33, 41, 42
Friedan, Betty, 62
Friedkin, William, 102
Fulci, Lucio, 46, 48, 76, 145
Furie, Sidney J., 65

Get Out, 120–26, 129
Ghost Hunters, 151
GI Bill of Rights (also known as the Servicemen's Readjustment Act), 12–13
Grave Secrets: The Legacy of Hilltop Drive, 144–45
Great Depression, 10, 11, 18

Halloween, 31
Haunted House, A, 66, 134–35
Haunted Mansion, The, 129–32
Haunting, The (1963), 57
Haunting, The (1999), 58, 133
Haunting of Hill House, The (book): and house as sentient being, 51–54, 56; and *The Legend of Hell House*, 56; and loneliness, 62; and psychological entrapment, 54; and *Rose Red*, 57–58; and the Suburban Gothic, 4, 31; and unresolved trauma, 33–34
Haunting of Hill House, The (Netflix, 2018): and the appeal of the Suburban

Gothic, 3; and bad mothers, 94–96; and flipping homes, 21; and home as sentient being, 50, 54–55; and horror narratives, 70; and nonlinear narratives, 151; and psychological entrapment, 54; and refusal to believe, 45–47; and vulnerable children, 110; and unresolved trauma, 33–34, 39–41

hauntology, 38

Hayden, Dolores: and debt, 16; and employer-designed housing options, 8; and gender in suburbia, 61–62; and housing prices, 15; and isolation, 44; and race in suburbia, 114; and suburban conformity, 13

Hereditary, 3, 48, 90–93

Holzer, Hans, 138–39

Home, 26–27, 93–94, 95

Home Loan Bank System, 10

Home Owners' Loan Corporation (HOLC), 10–11, 115–16

Hooper, Tobe, 31, 111, 119, 153

Hoover, Herbert, 10

Host, 159

House by the Cemetery, The, 46, 48, 76, 145

House Is Not a Home, A, 46, 126–28, 136

House on Haunted Hill (1999), 57

housing bubble, 18

I Am the Pretty Thing That Lives in the House, 72–73

Industrial Revolution 6, 7

Innkeepers, The, 48

Innocents, The, 4, 108–9

Insidious, 106–7

It: Chapter Two, 41–42, 48, 140

Jackson, Shirley: and adaptations of *Haunting of Hill House*, 3, 4, 33, 54; and Nandor Fodor, 42; and the *Haunting of Hill House* book, 51–54, 56; and loneliness, 62; and *Rose Red*, 57, 58, 59; and the Suburban Gothic, 31–32

James, Henry, 108

Jessabelle, 34

Kawash, Samira, 9

Kent, Jennifer, 5, 36, 80

King, Stephen: and *It*, 47–48; and *It: Chapter Two*, 140; and *Pet Sematary*, 140, 141–42; and *Rose Red*, 57–58; and *The Shining*, 55–56, 140; and suburbia, 31

Klein, Aaron, 16

Lam, Jeff, 26

Legend of Hell House, The, 56, 65, 133
Leni, Paul 2
Levin, Ira, 15
Levitt, William, 13
Levitt & Sons, 14
Levittown, 13, 14, 117, 118, 149
Lipsitz, George, 118
Lin, Frank, 26, 34
"Little Girl Lost," 112–13

Macy, Trevor, 39, 45, 50
Malicious: and domestic violence, 63; and parenting, 98–100; and race, 127, 136, 137
Matheson, Richard, 31–32, 112
McKamey Manor 1
Medak, Peter, 48, 133
Monster House, 50
Morgenson, Gretchen, 18
Mumford, Lewis, 14, 28, 44
Murphy, Eddie, 119–20, 129, 132
Murphy, Ryan, 20

Ngai, Sianne, 119, 146–47
Nixey, Troy, 20

Old Dark House, The, 2
Other Side of the Door, The, 96–97

Paranormal Activity, 134–35, 150, 151
Pet Sematary, 140, 141–42

Poe, Edgar Allan, 29, 49, 50
Poltergeist: and burial grounds, 143, 145; and references to, 86, 119, 133; and suburbia, 31; and technology, 153; and *The Twilight Zone,* 112; and vulnerable children, 111
predatory lending, 16, 17–18
Pulse, 154–56

Ramsay, Lynn, 80
Ray, Christopher, 46
redlining, 115
Ring, The, 151–54, 155, 157
Ringu, 151–52
Roosevelt, Franklin Delano, 10, 11
Rosenberg, Stuart, 22, 23
Rose Red, 57–59, 111, 151
Rothstein, Richard, 116–17
Rutkowski, Michael, 24

Saegert, Susan, 9
Scary Movie, 133
Scary Movie 2, 133–34
Schubart, Rikke, 79–80
Scream, 133
Scream 2, 133
Servicemen's Readjustment Act (also known as GI Bill of Rights), 12–13
Shelley, Mary, 29
Shining, The (book), 55, 72, 140
Shining, The (movie), 68, 140
Simard, François, 5, 140

Simmons, Laurie, 91
Sinister, 104
Sinister 2, 71, 104–6
Something Evil, 77
Spielberg, Steven, 58, 77
Spiral, 27–28
Stepford Wives, The, 15, 124, 125
Stoker, Bram, 29
Suburbicon, 118
Summer of 84, 1, 5, 140

Thing, The, 31
Turn of the Screw, The, 108
Twilight Zone, The, 112–13

Uninvited, The, 2, 5, 35–36

Visions, 76–77

Wan, James, 43, 48, 72, 106, 153
Webb, Gerald, 127, 128–29
We Need to Talk About Kevin, 80–82, 93
Whale, James 2
Whissell, Anouk, 5, 140
Whissell, Yoann-Karl, 5, 140
Wiese, Andrew, 117
Winchester House, 53, 58
Witch, The, 4, 100–102
Wood, Robin, 33
World War II, 6, 12, 31, 117, 148, 149

ABOUT THE AUTHOR

Dahlia Schweitzer is an associate professor at the Fashion Institute of Technology. Her previous works include *L.A. Private Eyes* (2019), *Going Viral: Zombies, Viruses, and the End of the World* (2018), *Cindy Sherman's Office Killer: Another Kind of Monster* (2014), and essays in publications including *Journal of Popular Film and Television*, *Jump Cut*, and *Journal of Popular Culture*.